to remember love

**two promises
that led me to
the notes
in the ashes**

lived and written by

Tonya Ferguson

Philippians 4:13

To Contact Tonya Ferguson

twitter: @Tonya_Ferguson

email: tonya@tonya-ferguson.com

website: www.tonya-ferguson.com

facebook page: Tonya Ferguson

music downloads: at amazon.com and itunes

Cover Designed By: Sheila Freeland of "The Design Seed"

Cover Created By: Songcatcher Productions

to remember love
two promises that led me to the notes in the ashes

Published By: Songcatcher Productions

ISBN 978-0-09847772-0-4

It's with a grateful heart I give all the Praise and Glory to my Precious Heavenly Father for carrying me through the times in my life that are written down on these pages.

I am so proud to be able to say that the first people to share the love of Jesus with me were my parents. I was so Blessed to have parents that not only encouraged me to dream, but insisted on it. Then they stood by me, as together we persevered, to make my dreams come true.

As far back as I can remember my mother had a dream of one day writing a book. She told the best stories when I was a child and I believe she really did have a book in her that needed to be written. How were any of us to know that before she would be able to fulfill her dream she would be dealt such a horribly, cruel blow? I guess in some ironic way my mom's dream did come true, but with one major twist. Instead of writing her book she "became" her book.

This book is dedicated to:

- My husband, Kevon, for being my greatest encourager at all times, my best friend, my Co-Caregiver and a tremendous Man Of God.

- My daughters, Chelsea and Lacy, for being my heart's smile, my Co-Caregivers, and for having the hearts of Jesus.

- My dad, Lee Walker, who taught me the importance of love, laughter, and family, by the way he lived his life out loud and to the fullest.

- My mom, Wilma Walker, who's love taught me to believe, who's wonderful imagination and story telling will forever live in my heart, and who deserves to have her dream come true most of all.

- My brother, John, his wife Renita, and children Katie and Timothy, for living the legacy our parents left behind with me.

the stepping stones of my journey

When I Can't See Tomorrow For Today

When I can't see tomorrow for today.
When sorrow always seems one step away.
When I doubt my strength He says just believe,
And He will make a way.
When I can't see tomorrow for today.

When I can't see tomorrow and my yesterday is gone.
And I fall into a valley unable to go on.
That's when He wraps His arms around me,
And He carries me on my way.
When I can't see tomorrow for today.

When I can't see tomorrow for today.
When I must stay instead of run away.
When it's too much to bear, when my heart starts to tear,
Then all I do is pray.
When I can't see tomorrow for today.

When I can't see tomorrow and my yesterday is gone.
And I fall into a valley unable to go on.
That's when He wraps His arms around me,
And He carries me on my way.
When I can't see tomorrow for today.

When I can't see tomorrow for today.
No matter how I feel I'll give Him praise.
When I don't know why, a sea of tears I must cry,
His Joy in me still stays.
When I can't see tomorrow for today.

When I can't see tomorrow and my yesterday is gone.
And I fall into a valley unable to go on.
That's when He wraps His arms around me,
And He carries me on my way.
When I can't see tomorrow for today.

believe

in

the

dark

what

you

learned

in

the

light

stone 1

my black hole

But I am like an olive tree,
thriving in the house of God.
I will always trust in God's unfailing love.
Psalm 52:8

∞ ∞ ∞

The words in this book were born out of a deep, black, bottomless hole that bore its way through my heart on January 13, 1998, at 7:57 a.m. A hole that went to the depths of my soul and will never be filled back in. A hole just as real and unexplainable as each unique sunrise that we experience every day. A hole always meant to be seen and felt, but never meant to consume, destroy or bury me in.

I've learned there are many things in my life I will question, but not all of my questions will have an answer for me to know right now. I just have to make peace with that fact even if I don't like it. The most difficult part of my journey was taking the first step. That step was taken on

January 13, 1998. Since then, all of my other steps have had no choice but to follow after that first one. Now I just have to keep walking to see where they are going to take me.

My intention is not for this to be a sad story, but an honest story. I want others to know it's not where you've been that matters, it's where you end up. The importance isn't just in the fact that you started the race, but that you finish it. There may be times you may not feel encouraged while you are reading this. That's because there were times it wasn't encouraging while I was living it. I'm just being honest with you.

At this very moment, I'm not even sure how it will end. I don't really see how there could be an "end." I guess because I'm not there yet. I am living this story as I put it down on paper. I'm living this one second at a time and one word at a time. Instead of there being an end, I may just come to a peaceful place in my heart and know that it is well with my soul. As I put in place the last word, on the last page, only then will I know where it ends. All the while knowing there's much more traveling I will have yet to do.

In the telling of my story, it is not my desire to list all the stages of grief in a nice neat order. I won't be telling you what you should or should not do if you lose a loved one. I will not be talking about support groups or tell you how you must cope with the loss of a loved one. I'm sure you know the type of books I'm talking about. The ones that are so clinical they reek of disinfectant. No, my aim is not for this to be a "HOW-TO" book at all. If I've learned anything from my experience, it's that there are no rules. I simply want to share my real-life experience with others in a real-life way. I want to give you Hope to replace your Hopelessness. I want to give you Glory to replace your Grief. I want to give you Blessings to replace your Battles. I want to give you Faith to replace your Fear.

I want to approach this subject from a different perspective, looking from the inside out, so to speak. I want to breathe life into grief because life is what we must continue to live as we battle through our grief. I want to remove the veil of mystery from a subject few want to talk about. So many books make you feel worse instead of better. You're made to feel like you will flunk their course if you don't follow the steps in their book, in the order they list them, and in a timely fashion, thank you very much. I'm here to tell you right now, THERE IS NO PROTOCOL FOR DEATH OR LOSS. It is a very personal thing for each and every person to deal with. There are no winners or losers in this game called grief.

Before this happened to me, I had read a few things on the subject. If I am to be honest, however, I'd have to say I read it mostly out of curiosity. After my loss, I didn't feel like the things I had read covered the experience in a very real way. There are no rules and no way of doing things wrong.

I have found out there's no set time frame I've been able to fit my grief into. So, no matter how inconvenient it may be for those around me, that's just the way it has to be.

If I've learned anything at all, it's that this is bigger than me.

Each person must make their own way through their own nightmare. They must force themselves to not allow those around them to make them feel bad for what they're feeling or doing. People mean well, but they can actually make you feel worse instead of better sometimes.

I never had a clue how I would react to something like this. I'm not sure I can explain even after living it. I only know I want others who may feel some of the things I feel, or act some of the ways I do, to know they're not alone. Not all of our reactions during this time may be "textbook" in the way we handle them, but that doesn't make us wrong or abnormal in our experience. What it makes us is REAL. Believe me, having a loss this great in my life made me understand the word "REAL."

Through my journey there have been those around me that have acted like there was some mystical, magical list that I should follow. They tried to convince me that if I would follow this list everything would be peachy-keen. If there is such a list, I have yet to find it. If I could find it I probably would start a bonfire with it.

I've always liked the feeling of being able to fix whatever was going wrong in my life. If I had to classify myself, I would say I was a consummate "handyman" when it came to fixing my life's problems. However, there's one thing I've had to learn the hard way in this journey. I've learned that sometimes I just can't have all my ducks in a row. No matter how hard I try. That makes for a very uneasy feeling for me to have to deal with. Just about the time I get my ducks all lined up, someone picks up a gun and starts shooting them.

No matter how hard I try, I'm unable to "organize" this experience in my life. There isn't a file cabinet big enough to file this away. I feel like I'm sitting in a tiny rowboat in the middle of a huge ocean and I don't have any oars. I'm at the mercy of everything going on around me and I have absolutely no control of the situation at all. What a helpless, hopeless feeling.

No one likes to feel in control more than I do. One of the most difficult things I've had to come to terms with was the fact there was something in my life I wasn't able to control, and I don't like it. I DON'T LIKE IT AT ALL.

In writing this book, it is my sincere prayer that sharing this most intimate and painful experience with others, not only helps someone else, but also helps me. I really pray it helps me.

For I can do everything through Christ,

who gives me strength.

Philippians 4:13

stone 2

love in the cracked ivories

Before the mountains were born,
before you gave birth to the earth and the world,
from beginning to end, you are God.
Psalm 90:2

∞ ∞ ∞

My family has always been extremely close. None of us ever had to wonder if we were loved, because there was never a day that went by that we didn't hear the words "I Love You."

There were four of us in my family: my dad, my mom, my brother, John and me. I truly feel there were no two parents anywhere that could have loved their children more than my parents did. No matter what John and I desired to do, they were always behind us 100%. There was nothing about our parents that could have made them fit into the category of "most parents." They were completely unique and very "hands-on." Love and laughter bathed our home and our lives daily.

Our house was the one that our friends always wanted to come to. Many times our friends even went with us on vacations. Even our friends felt the love from our mom and dad. Our parents treated our friends just like their own children. Dad would always tease and pick on my girlfriends, and they loved it. If he teased with you, then he liked you.

I can remember my dad's 40th birthday. We gave him a surprise party and all the guests were our friends, not adults, but kids.

We were raised in a musical family and began sharing our musical gifts in church at a very young age. I was singing songs with my dad at the age of two. I was playing guitar at the age of seven. Then, two weeks before my thirteenth birthday I walked across the room one day and told my dad if he would get me a piano, I would learn how to play it. Now keep in mind, I had never touched a piano or ever expressed any desire to play one, up to that point. Most parents would have laughed it off with a big old, "Yeah Right," but like I've said, my parents weren't like most parents.

The next day my dad was in a little grandma's house and saw a big, old, upright piano sitting in her basement. The kind of piano that takes ten men to move. He bought the piano that very day and brought it home. Every other key had part of the ivory missing or it was cracked, but I loved that piano.

The only thing I had in the house was a church hymnal.

When I picked it up it fell open to the song, "I'll Fly Away." It was my dad's favorite. So I sat down and began to teach myself the chords on the piano that I knew from the guitar. Within two weeks I was PLAYING that piano like I'd taken lessons for years. There is no explanation other than God. From the moment my fingers touched those broken and cracked ivory keys, I could play that piano.

My parents could tell something supernatural was taking place, so on my thirteenth birthday in rolled a brand new beautiful piano. I would play and sing for hours and just get lost in the music. My first public singing debut was in our church, when I was thirteen years old, with my dad sitting beside me on the piano bench, singing with me.

It wasn't long before John and I realized that music was taking over a huge portion of our hearts. We never took music lessons. God gave us our talents and musical gifts, they weren't learned from books. We never really felt like we had a choice when it came to music. It just seemed to have a hold on us. It was in the blood that coursed through our veins.

Mom and Dad were there every time we played or sang. We always knew they'd be out there cheering us on. It wasn't long before John and I developed a mutual dream: we wanted to have our own family country music show.

I'll never forget the day we told mom about our dream. We were at home, in our music room, when we started telling her about our dream of having our own show. Now, "most" mothers probably would have said, "That's nice kids," and sent us on our way. However, our mother wasn't like "most" mothers; she reacted in an entirely different way.

When John and I told her about our dream she did something that proved to me the depth of her love for us. She got up and got a file folder, some paper, and a pen. She proceeded to quickly write down everything we were telling her. That day she wrote with the same enthusiasm she used to write our letters to Santa many, many years ago. We talked and laughed together for a long time that day. That was a very special day in my memory. When we were finished, we not only had the location for our music show, we had the name. We decided to name it "Kin-Fokes Country Music Show." You see, even in our dream to have a show, our family still came first.

Mom told Dad later on that evening and it didn't surprise him in the least. It was the topic of our dinner conversation that night and several nights after that. Little did we know it would ever turn into something more than a file folder that Mom made so very special to us that day in the music room.

Time went by and I married, but not before John made sure Kevon had mastered the bass guitar. John said we needed a bass player for our show, so they spent our entire courtship playing music together. About six or seven months after our wedding, Mom and Dad sold their business, little farm, and auctioned off everything they didn't want to take with them. You guessed it! They were going to make our dream come true.

I'm not sure I will ever be able to express to anyone how that made us feel. Most children know their parents love them and believe in them. What our parents were willing to do for us, however, went way beyond the "call of duty" for any parent. For them to completely give up everything they had worked for their entire lives, so we could reach for our dream, means more to me than words will ever be able to express. There's no way to ever give back to them what they gave up for us. I honestly feel like if there was such a thing as loving so much that it hurt, my mother and father would have lived their lives in excruciating pain.

Our dream did come true. We lived it for sixteen years, in two different locations. Our season ran six nights a week for six months, every year.

It was during one of those show seasons that John met his wife, Renita. She came to watch the show one evening and later that summer John saw her in town and they started talking. The rest is history. She became a part of our family and our show by running our ticket office, selling our merchandise, and working in our motel.

After our daughters, Chelsea and Lacy, and John and Renita's children, Katie and Timothy, came along, our "family" was at last complete. Those four children became the very breath their Nanny and Papa breathed. The four of them gave us all a whole new meaning for the word "Love." Each one of them had their Papa wrapped tightly around their little finger, and he wouldn't have had it any other way. We always accused Dad of not having the word "no" in his vocabulary when it came to the grandchildren. Don't think for one moment that death only affects the adults in a family. Their little tears fell just like our tears did. Their little hearts broke just like our hearts did. They just didn't have the ability to articulate it very well. They may process it all differently, but the pain is still the same.

I feel so fortunate to be able to say my whole family has lived together, played together, laughed together, cried together, and loved together. I don't know how many times Dad said, "If one of us hurts, we all hurt. If one of us is happy, we're all happy. That's what family is all about." That's why our show was so special to us. It was one more thing we could all do together as a family. Every night as we performed, we gave a little piece of our hearts away to the crowd. Our hearts were where the music came from. We weren't just acting like we were having a good time on stage, we WERE having a good time. The people that came to our show could certainly tell the difference. We weren't simply performers. They would tell us they really felt like they were one of the Kin-Fokes, at the end of our show.

We had people that would come back year after year to see our show. They would bring family and friends with them and introduce them to us, and thought we should be able to remember them because they felt as close to us as family. We had one dear couple that came just about every week-end for years. They even had their own seats they sat in. People would even come and bring us gifts they had made for us to display in our theater. Some folks even came to see us in the off-season when our show was closed for the winter. I think it was because we were all extremely approachable and made everyone feel so comfortable. We always treated our folks like Kings and Queens when they came through our doors.

We were very picky about the music we played. We wouldn't do the "traditional" beer drinking, cheating kind of country songs. If we couldn't sing it in front of our own children and sing it from our hearts, then we didn't sing it at all. We did a variety of old and new country, bluegrass, and always ended with gospel and patriotic music. Sprinkled throughout the show was fun, Hillbilly, Ozark comedy, generously provided by my mom and dad, who were also know as, Aunt Polly and Pappy. My mother did a beautiful rendition of "The Three Rusty Nails," recitation at the end of every show. For sixteen years, it made grown men cry. I can remember one night we had a whole tour bus full of young people from France in the audience. They couldn't speak a bit of english, but they had a blast.

One of the most heart-wrenching things I had to do, just a couple of weeks after losing my dad, was walk across our stage, reach up and take his microphone out of the stand, and pack it away. I couldn't believe that in one single heartbeat it was all over. Sixteen years was over in an instant. Never again would we stand as a family, lined up across our stage and make music, magic and memories together. Never again. Never again would we ever stand as a family and do anything together. Never again.

For I can do everything through Christ,

who gives me strength.

Philippians 4:13

stone 3

his last day

Lord, remind me how brief my time on earth will be.
Remind me that my days are numbered, how fleeting my life is.
Psalm 39:4

My black hole really began on Monday evening, January 12, 1998. I wasn't even close to being prepared for the kind of sadness I was about to walk into. I'm not talking about the kind of sadness you might feel if you lost your wedding ring, got fired from your job, your dog ran away, or you had to move away from all of your friends and family. The kind of sadness I'm talking about doesn't even have a definition listed in the dictionary. I think it's because there really aren't any words that can describe this type of sadness. You see, this kind of sadness permeates every fiber of your being, from the top of your head to the tips of your toes. It becomes as much a part of you as the very beating of your heart. It becomes your every breath. That's the kind of sadness I'm talking about.

That evening Kevon, Lacy, and I dropped Chelsea off at Mom and Dad's to spend the night and then we went out for dinner. As we were just beginning to eat I heard an ambulance scream past the restaurant. Of all the ambulances I'd seen go by before, this one was different. I knew something was wrong. My stomach began to churn. Within seconds, the phone rang at the register. Suddenly, I heard a woman's voice yelling my name out as if she were taking roll call. Inside I began screaming, "I knew it, I knew it!" As I put the phone to my ear I didn't know who would be on the other end and I didn't know if anything would come out of my mouth. I must have made a noise, because it was then I heard my mom say, "Tonya, I need You." Very calmly, almost like I had rehearsed it I asked, "Are you at home?" She said, "Yes." The calmness in our voices was almost sickening. Even then, I think we both knew what was ahead.

As I told my mom that I would be right there, time came to a screeching halt. I began motioning for Kevon and Lacy to get up, as I was trying to write out a check for the meal we had just begun to eat. I don't remember getting in the car, all I remember was telling Kevon to hurry, hurry, and to take the back way to my parent's house. I wasn't crying or yelling, but I do remember praying as I rubbed my hands together trying to feel my fingers. My fingers were just the first of many things that would go numb that night.

As we rounded the corner I could see the lights from the

ambulance flashing before we ever got to the house. Vehicles were lined up and down both sides of the street as far as I could see. Our car hadn't even come to a stop before I threw open the door, jumped out and started running across the yard and into the front door. I stood there amazed at all the people crowded into my parent's house. I didn't know anyone that was there. I kept scanning the room for a familiar face and then I looked down on the floor. There was my dad, lying unconscious in front of the TV, on the floor. The light gray sweatshirt I had just given him for Christmas a couple of weeks before was cut off of him and laying beside him.

I couldn't get close enough to him, so I ran out of the front door and came in the kitchen door. There I could reach down and touch his feet. Mom came out of the bedroom for just a second, got Lacy, and took her back to the bedroom with her and Chelsea. The police officer tried to get me to go into the bedroom, but I couldn't. I wouldn't. I looked at their table. Their dinner, their "last" dinner together, was sitting there. Only one bite had been taken out of my dad's food. The table was now shoved into the corner to give them more room for all of their medical equipment.

Later, my mother told me about the last moments of my dad's life. She said she was cooking dinner when he came bounding in the house smiling and telling her what a wonderful day it had been. He washed his hands and went into say hello to Chelsea. She was having her dinner in bed while she watched a show. He teased her about how nice it must be to be served dinner in bed like a princess. He closed the door and sat down at the table. Mom told him she was making omelets for dinner and asked if he was hungry. He said he was starving and that omelets sounded great. She set the plates on the table and sat down. As they held hands that night, they prayed what would be their last prayer together. He picked up his fork, took one bite and said, "Babe, this is the best omelet I've ever tasted." As the last word escaped his lips he slumped over to the right in his chair. My mom thought he was being silly and told him to stop. Then she realized something was really wrong. She screamed for Chelsea to come help her. Mom had Chelsea hold dad so he wouldn't fall out of his chair as she called 911. She called me and John and then they held him until the ambulance got there. So, on my dad's last day on this earth, he was Happy, he was Blessed, he Prayed, and on my dad's last day he was Loved.

As I watched the paramedics perform CPR on my dad, I was surprised at how different it looked than on TV. I found myself almost hypnotized by the rhythm of the compressions. It was then my brother, John came rushing in the kitchen door. As I looked at his pale face and into his hopeful eyes, we both knew. In the same way you would talk very gingerly to a small child, and with a sweet smile on his face as if to reassure me that he would be ok with whatever my answer would be, he whispered, "Is he gone?" "No," I said, "They're working on him."

This whole time I remember hearing orders being barked out amongst all the men there. It was then that I heard someone ask if anyone knew his name. *What? How dare they I thought*. How dare they not know his name. After all, that was my dad. All of a sudden a voice rang out above all the commotion. "His name is Lee Walker." At the same time that very authoritative voice was echoing off of every wall in the house, I realized that voice was mine.

As John, Kevon, and I stood huddled together, arm in arm, I saw one of the guys reach for the paddles. You know, the things they use to shock someone with when their heart has stopped beating. It was at that very moment I knew my family would be forever changed. Forever changed.

The waiting was torturous. Why was time standing still? I just wanted someone to tell us something. Was he or wasn't he gone? They stopped shocking him. No one was saying anything. The house was full of all these people and yet the quiet is all I could hear. I looked around and everyone was getting their things together, but no one was telling us anything. I looked at the police officer and asked him if our dad was alive or not. He looked at me and half-whispered, "They said they have a faint pulse. They're going to take him to the hospital." Isn't it odd that he would whisper at a time like that?

Everyone and everything seemed eerily quiet. I couldn't even hear myself breathing. Maybe I wasn't. It's almost as if we think the softer we speak of death and dying the less real

"IT," (death), will somehow be. We simply refuse to acknowledge it out loud because it might make it become real. So, we whisper, mouth the words, or try to speak with our eyes. Anything but talk out loud. We must remain cushioned by the silence at all times. I think we feel that within the silence "IT" won't find us.

For I can do everything through Christ,

who gives me strength.

Philippians 4:13

stone 4

unselfish prayers

And the Holy Spirit helps us in our weakness. For example, we don't know what God wants us to pray for. But the Holy Spirit prays for us with groanings that cannot be expressed in words. And the Father who knows all hearts knows what the Spirit is saying, for the Spirit pleads for us believers in harmony with God's own will.
Romans 8:26-27

In one simple second we all began to scatter. All I know was I ended up with my mom and daughters in her car on our way to the hospital.

There wasn't much talking taking place while I was driving. The tears in my eyes caused all the headlights of the oncoming cars to be blurred. Mom asked me if I thought dad was very bad and if I thought he would make it. I told her I didn't think it looked very good, but I think we both already knew that. I think we were just trying to fill the silence in the car with something. I really think we were just trying to keep "IT" away.

When we arrived at the hospital emergency room they asked us some questions, then brought out a bag and started removing the articles one by one, very mechanically. As they took each item out, they made a list of my dad's personal things he had on him when he was brought in. The last thing they handed me was my dad's wedding ring. I never thought I would ever see that ring off of his finger. In all of my life it had never left his left hand.

We asked them if they could tell us how he was. They left for a second, came back and told us we should wait in this little room, and that the doctor would come and talk to us as soon as he could. I looked to my left at the closed door of that little room. "NO, not the little room," I screamed inside my head. They only tell you to go in there if they're going to tell you something awful and they want you to be somewhere private. I didn't want to go in that little room. I didn't want to hear the awful things the doctor was going to tell us. "IT" would surely find us in there.

By now, everyone else was there including our Pastor and some friends. We all waited. We waited for what seemed like an eternity. We were afraid to be hopeful. We were afraid not to be hopeful. We wanted the doctor to come. We didn't want the doctor to come. We sat there trying to get prepared for what he might tell us. It seemed like everything was moving in slow-motion as the doctor walked into that little room. To this day, I'm not real sure of the exact words the doctor did say. He didn't seem too concerned about much of anything. He was very cold and nonchalant. He told us they had to shock him a few more times in the emergency room, that he had a heartbeat, that he never had regained conciousness, that they had put him on a ventilator and that they were moving him. We asked if dad was going to make it and he said we didn't have to give up hope..."yet." That word rang out over and over like an echo in a cavern. He said we would have to wait and see if he made it through the night. He seemed quite unconcerned and uncaring about the whole situation.

As we walked down the hall to yet another waiting room, it didn't even feel like my feet were touching the floor, much less propelling me further into this nightmare. At that moment I couldn't feel anything. Little did we know then, a nightmare was exactly what we were blindly walking into.

We sat and waited until someone came and told us we could go in and see him, BUT, they wanted to prepare us for what we were going to see. Prepare? Why would they possibly need to prepare me to see my dad? Many times we had seen IV tubes and EKG monitors. It was the ventilator. That was something we hadn't seen on him before. Now, don't get me wrong. Ventilators are a wonderful thing, but they can also be one of the most terrifying things to see attached to your loved one. Along with the constant swishing sound it made, there were the screaming alarms that would go off every time my dad would cough or fight against the ventilator with his own respirations. I think I hated watching that more than anything. It was horrible to see him struggle against that machine. He appeared to be gagging and almost in a seizure type of behavior during those times of struggling.

We talked to another doctor, who told us things like, he doesn't respond to pain stimuli, his pupils don't seem to be reactive, and we're not sure if there is any brain activity. He said we could stay with him if we wanted and that the next twenty-four hours would tell us more. If he survived the night there would be testing done on his brain the next day. How horrible it was for us to have to live the next twelve hours based on "IF."

I went and got the girls so they could go in and see their Papa, possibly for the last time. We all went in and told Dad that we were there. We told him what was happening. The nurse told us to talk to him and not to be afraid to touch him. The nurse said they couldn't tell us that Dad wasn't able to hear us. They didn't have to tell me that, I knew he could hear us. I knew he could feel our love.

The girls didn't want to stay very long, so I took them to a waiting room where they could have some privacy. I went out to the waiting room our friends were in so I could give them a progress report, and then we all just sat and waited. We waited to see how drastic our world was going to be changed. We waited to see if our family was getting ready to become one less. We waited to see just how big a hole we would be left to live with. We just waited.

Again, everyone seemed to try and chase away the deafening silence with chit-chat. We all smiled at each other trying to comfort each other. It just wasn't time for "IT" to come yet.

After a few hours everyone left except our family. We all tried to reassure each other with positive comments, hugs and prayers. Everyone was being strong for each other. It had all happened so fast that evening, I think we were all just floating around in a dark gray cloud of shock.

We all went in and out of dad's room for hours that night. At around 3:00 a.m. John said he needed to run home and check on his family because some of them had been sick. Kevon needed to run home and let our dog out. Mom needed to go home and get on some different clothes, and we decided to send the girls home with her so they could go to bed. I told everone I would stay at the hospital so they all could do what they needed to do and I would keep them posted if there were any changes.

I was surprised by the eerie calmness that had fallen on all of us that night. A calmness that seemed as comforting as having a warm, fuzzy blanket wrapped around you on a cold, winter's night.

Right now, seems as good a time as any, to talk about prayer. Yes, there was non-stop praying taking place that night, from several people. There was one person's prayers however, that surprised me more that anyone else's that night. Those prayers were mine. Before this horrible event had happened I had always wondered how I would react in this kind of situation. I had wondered what my prayers would be like. To tell you the truth, it's times like these we all want to be selfish. We want what WE want.

I walked my family out of the hospital. As they drove away into the darkness, I had to stop and look up at the beautiful sky, stars, and moon. Even with darkness trying to consume my life, I still revelled at God's beauty and the magnificance of His creation, that was so evident and all around me.

As I stood there alone, I began to pray. The tears streamed down my face as I spoke my heart to my Precious Lord. I prayed like I've never prayed before, but not once did I ask God to do what I wanted Him to do. I couldn't believe that. Of all the times I had prayed for something, this should have been the time for me to have asked for what I wanted. I couldn't though, it just would have been wrong, and I knew that. In my spirit, I knew that.

I absolutely wanted my dad to live. I wanted to hear him say I Love You for many years to come. I wanted to hear him laugh for many years to come. I wanted to feel his arms wrapped around me giving me one of those special hugs for many years to come. I wanted, I wanted, I wanted. However, for once it wasn't going to matter what I wanted and I knew that. I knew I had to turn this one completely over to God and be willing to accept the fact that this was not catching Him by surprise. His plans were made for each one of us before we were ever born. I knew I wouldn't have a problem with the turning it over part, but the willing to accept it part scared me to the depths of my soul.

I went back into the waiting room and a nurse came out and told me I could go in and see my dad. I didn't want him to be with strangers. I didn't want him to be alone. I wanted us there with him if "IT" was going to come.

As I looked at my dad, I couldn't help but wonder what was going to happen. It was then that I noticed there seemed to be an uneasiness in him. That's the best way I can describe it, an uneasiness. There was a battle going on inside him. I could see it. I could feel it. It broke my heart. I knew I had to do anything I could to try to put him at ease.

For I can do everything through Christ,

who gives me strength.

Philippians 4:13

stone 5

first promise made

Take care of any widow who has no one else to care for her. But if she has children or grandchildren, their first responsibility is to show godliness at home and repay their parents by taking care of them. This is something that pleases God.

1 Timothy 5:3-4

∞ ∞ ∞

I bent over and kissed my dad on the cheek, ran my hand over his head, and whispered in his ear how much I loved him. I took his hand and squeezed it, hoping he would squeeze mine back. I always thought my dad had the strongest, yet gentlest hands I'd ever seen. As I held his hand to my cheek and my tears ran over his fingers, I began to think about our goodnight ritual from the time I was a little, bitty girl. Every night when I went to tell him goodnight and that I loved him, he would "tweak" my nose as he told me he loved me. One of the sweetest memories I will carry with me forever, is of my dad tweaking my nose and telling me he loved me the night before I got married. I couldn't bare the thought of him never being able to do that again.

As I laid my head on his chest and put my arms around him I began to share my heart with him. I told him there was a song I sang one year on our show called "Daddy's Hands," and that I always felt the person who wrote those lyrics must have crawled inside my heart to get them. I leaned forward and sang it quietly into his ear.

I talked and cried and prayed for a long time. I told him everything you can imagine you would have said in that same moment. I relived my life as I talked to him in those early morning hours. I told him he had fought long and hard, and that he wasn't losing the battle, he was finally going to get his great reward. I told him not to worry about Mom or any of his family because he was the one that taught us how to take care of each other, and that's exactly what we would do. We would always take care of each other. I **"PROMISED"** him that I would take care of mom for the rest of her life. I told him that we would all be ok. I wanted to take away any worries he might have about leaving us. I didn't want him to feel guilty. I told him he could rest now and everything would be ok. I told him how much he meant to all of us as a husband, father, father-in-law, and most importantly, the world's most special Papa. I told him he didn't have to hold on any longer because I knew he was very tired. I told him he could go be with Jesus.

I no more than finished that sentence when, suddenly, alarms started going off. Nurses rushed in and yelled at me to get out. I asked them if it was bad and they said yes. One of the nurses walked me out of the room and told me that he would come and tell me what was going on as soon as he could. I reached out and grabbed a hold of his arm and pleaded with him not to let my dad die all alone. If he was going to die I wanted him to come and get me so I could be in there with him. He assured me he would, and then he turned and walked back into the room.

That was the first time during this whole ordeal I wanted to run as fast as I could and scream as loud as I could to try and make it all go away. I felt like I was almost in a panic. I stood there crying, flinging my hands and praying. I waited for them to come out and tell me if I should call the rest of my family to come back to the hospital. I felt so utterly helpless. I felt so utterly useless. I felt so utterly desperate. I felt so utterely lost. I felt so utterly broken.

Finally the nurse came out. He took my hand and looked into my eyes with a regret I've never seen before. In a very calm voice he said, "We got him back, but we've had to shock your dad over fifteen times. The doctor said to tell you there's really nothing else we can do, you'd better call your family."

Suddenly, I couldn't breathe. I couldn't speak. All I could hear was my heartbeating in my ears. Then I noticed a tear rolling down his face. I was shocked. I didn't think medical staff got emotional. They see so much. I thought they were calloused to death.

He grabbed both of my hands and as the tears rolled down his face he said, "I'm so sorry. We sure can tell that you all are a very strong and special family." As he walked away I picked up the receiver of the phone and made the three most painful and difficult phone calls of my life. One to my husband, one to my brother, and one to my mother. I had to tell them that "IT" was on the way.

As I finished another prayer, I went to be with my dad and wait for my the family to get there. As I held him, I cried. I wasn't crying for him, I was crying for me. My heart was breaking for what I knew I would no longer have.

I found it somewhat ironic that his arms are what welcomed me into this world and my arms would be what held him as he left this world. I wanted him to have peace in his leaving. I wanted him to know how proud I was to have had him in my life as my dad. I wanted him to know he could go, knowing we would always take care of each other. Just as he had done for all of us our entire lives.

I never would have dreamed, having time like this at someone's bedside, would have even come close to being a comfort. Yet, to this day, I feel drawn to that time in my mind when I'm feeling my worst. Not that all my memories of that time and place are pleasant ones, because they aren't. I can't even begin to count the nights that I was unable to sleep for hearing the swishing sound of that ventilator in my head. I would lay my head down on my pillow and as soon as I would close my eyes and get still I would hear that sound in my head. I would open my eyes and tell myself to stop thinking about that. As soon as I would try to close my eyes again, that sound was there.

For I can do everything through Christ,
who gives me strength.
Philippians 4:13

stone 6

liquid love

You keep track of all my sorrows.
You have collected all my tears in your bottle.
You have recorded each one in your book.
Psalm 56:8

∞ ∞ ∞

My family all entered at the same time and we all fell into each other's arms. At Dad's bedside were the four of us, our Pastor, and a friend of our's that was like the brother my dad never had. I can't express just how wonderful it is to have such a loving and merciful God to see us through times like these. He knows what we really need and provides it in such inconspicuous ways sometimes. He must have known we were going to need more support than what we already had, because in walked two nurses that had been there all night long. It was a man and a woman. We basically knew what a nurse's duties should include, and yes those duties were performed. However, it didn't take long for us to see these nurses were different. Their eyes were different. Their touch was different. Their words to us were different.

I understand why most doctors and nurses become somewhat hardened over time to situations like this. They have to be able to perform the duties they're required to do without becoming emotional. I think that's what made these nurses so special. There was still true compassion in their eyes. They wanted to do anything they could to make things easier for us. The male nurse told us he actually knew Dad and had been to our show. We had no idea they knew each other. He said they had coffee together every morning at the local coffee shop and that he really thought a lot of Dad. He also told us he had just lost his own father just six weeks before and had come to realize that tears like we were shedding, were nothing but pure "Liquid Love." What a beautiful word picture that painted in my mind. Now, tell me God was not orchestrating this whole ordeal.

Both of the nurses were constanly monitoring dad and consoling us. They told us what to expect at the end and they never left our sides until it was over. As we all took each other's hand so our Pastor could have a final prayer, the nurses reached out their hands and joined our circle. I couldn't believe it. Now that's something you don't see very often. My whole family was touched beyond words.

We were all gathered around my dad and were telling him what was in our hearts. We'd talk a little and cry a little. We'd talk a lot and cry a lot. All of us told him we knew it was time for him to go and that it was ok for him to turn loose. We told him he didn't have to try to hold on any longer. We were all giving him our Blessing to go be with Jesus. We were as ready as we were ever going to be and we knew he was certainly ready.

One of the last things I did was to bend over and sing one last song in my dad's ear, just for him. Even though he couldn't show it on his face, I could sense a smile in his spirit. It's not something I planned, I wasn't even thinking about it. It was the first song I taught myself on the piano, and it was dad's favorite gospel song. I don't think we could begin to count the times dad sang it with us as a group in churches and on our music show. So, as we all held him and loved him, I softly sang, "I'll Fly Away" to him for the last time.

Some glad morning when this life is o'er, I'll Fly Away.
To a home on God's celestial shore, I'll Fly Away.
I'll Fly Away Old Glory, I'll Fly Away.
When I die Hallelujah by and by, I'll Fly Away.

When the shadows of this life have gone, I'll Fly Away.
Like a bird from prison bars has flown, I'll Fly Away.
I'll Fly Away Old Glory, I'll Fly Away.
When I die Hallelujah by and by, I'll Fly Away.

The nurses were so good to make us aware of everything that was going on. Suddenly, I noticed the alarm wasn't going off on the ventilator anymore and dad wasn't fighting to breathe anymore. I looked at the nurse and she said the machine was doing all the breathing for Dad now and that he wasn't breathing on his own. At that moment we all knew dad had finally started to turn loose and was getting ready to go "HOME." I looked up at the machine that was monitoring his heartbeat. The nurse said there was still some activity, not actually a strong beat, but it was like his heart was quivering like jello. We all held on tighter to him and a desperation seemed to fall over all of us in those last final moments. It almost felt like we were afraid he might not have heard everything we 'd been saying to him all night long. We all started talking to him at the same time and our voices got louder and louder. It was as if we were watching sand run out of an hour glass. The fewer grains of sand left in the top the more desperate we became to tell him how much we loved him and that we knew he really didn't want to leave us, but that it would just be for a little while. About that time the nurse told us it was almost over. We were all beginning to fall apart by then. We knew "IT," (death), was knocking at the door. We wanted to scream for it to go away because we really weren't ready, but we couldn't. At that moment dad opened the door and allowed "IT" to come in. All of a sudden, above all the shouting and crying, I heard the nurse very calmly say, "7:57 a.m." He walked over, turned off the machine and he opened the blinds to the window. A yellow glow filled the room. We had not seen sunshine in two weeks until that very moment he opened the blinds. Everything was silent. Utterly, excruciatingly, SILENT. Who knew SILENCE could be so extraordinarily loud.

I looked up to see the two nurses that were with us wiping the tears from their eyes. The female nurse said if we wanted to step out she would remove all the machines, wires, etc. that were attached to him and then we could come back in and see him again. I told her to be really careful when she took off all the tape and sticky patches because his skin was thin and would tear easily because of a blood thinner he was on. Even though he was gone, I was still trying to take care of him.

The male nurse led us out and took us to the waiting room and said he was going to make us a fresh pot of coffee. We knew his shift had been over for quite some time. We told him he should be off work and already home. He told us he wasn't leaving us.

We all went back into Dad's room. I was so glad the nurse did that for us. It was a comfort to get to see dad without all the tubes and wires and machines. At last I could see a peacefulness on his face. It just seemed like moments had passed, when the men from the funeral home arrived to pick up my Dad's body. We stepped out into the hall and waited. As they rolled his completely covered body past us I reached out and touched one of the men's arms. I told him to please make sure they treated our dad's body with the respect he deserved.

As we walked out of the hospital that morning we all couldn't help but bask in the gloriousness of the sun as we walked across the parking lot. It was like a warm, sunny smile from dad, wrapping itself around each one of us, in what was the very darkest time in our lives. I couldn't help but look up towards Heaven and smile. God's Love, Grace, and Mercy was so evident to me as I got in the car all by myself. I couldn't imagine having to go through that night without God carrying me along the way. What a Mighty God we serve.

For I can do everything through Christ,

who gives me strength.

Philippians 4:13

stone 7

the final curtain

And since we died with Christ,
we know we will also live with him.
Romans 6:8

As soon as we got to my mother's house from the hospital the man from the funeral home was there to pick up Dad's clothes for his body to be buried in. It was then that he told us what time to come to the funeral home to "make the final arrangements." We went, made the decisions that needed to be made, and left.

I've never been a fan of funerals, and I'm still not. However, I do see how they can be beneficial in giving the family something to do. They tell you where and when to go. At a time like this your brain just shifts into neutral. I couldn't think. I couldn't function. I couldn't even occupy my own time.

One of my first memories I recalled during this time,

was the feeling that swept over me when I walked into my daughter's rooms and realized I was picking out their clothes to wear to my dad's funeral. The clothes they would wear to their dear Papa's funeral. It literally took my breath away.

The funeral seemed to give me an agenda. I had people telling me where I needed to be and when to be there. My time was taken up with important things to do and I didn't have to think of them on my own. After it was all over I almost missed having that type of structure in my life. I needed that busyness to keep me going. I didn't want anyone to put a period at the end of that sentence in my life. I didn't know where I would go from there. How would my life ever be normal again?

Everyone was very kind to us. I found it odd that I felt a source of peacefulness at the visitation service the night before the funeral. However, I felt sorry for the people that were around us. You could see them stumbling for words when they would walk up to us. We all know there's really nothing anyone can say to make it better, but for some reason people feel very uncomfortable with silence. They feel they must say something to make the silence go away. Some of their words were comforting to me and some were just simply disturbing.

I absolutely loved the fact that during Dad's funeral laughter erupted several times. Yes, laughter. He would have really gotten a kick out of that. No one enjoyed a good laugh more than my dad. Many of my childhood mornings began with his laughter, because he would wake me up by giving me a "wet willy" and then roar with laughter.

Something I heard my dad say several times throughout my life was that he wanted fast piano music and a fast hearse at his funeral. So that's what we did. I asked the Pastor to make an announcement. I wanted anyone that was going to be driving in the funeral procession, going to the cemetary, to lay on their horn all the way through the four way stoplight and as they passed our theater building. The hearse that carried my dad's body was the first one to sound its horn. It was awesome. My dad would have loved that. You could hear one continuous sound of horns for miles.

The graveside service was the toughest for me personally. It was also the shortest part of the whole funeral. I found it extremely difficult to leave the casket. My brother and I were the last ones to go. As we walked away we both leaned over and left one final kiss.

Once everything was over and everyone went home, I was left to carry on by myself. I was left to begin to discover what my "new normal" would be like. That's when I really found out just what I was made of. Discovering how I'd react every time I left my house and had to pass the cemetary just to get to town. Then getting to town and seeing our big theater building glaring at me like a huge tombstone. Or finding out how I'd feel to see the mound of flowers on top of his grave. Or to drive by and see the dead flowers removed leaving a rectangular piece of ground where no grass was growing. I felt such a complete sense of sadness. Just deep, deep sadness.

As I began to write all the Thank You notes and find a place to put all the beautiful live plants, I became painfully aware of just how many lives my dad had touched. I desperately hoped he had some idea of that when he was alive. Maybe that should be a lesson to all of us. Let those in your life know what they mean to you when it really counts and matters. Tell them when you can see their reaction with your own two eyes. Not when they're gone and an empty body is laying in a casket.

We never doubted how much we meant to my dad. He told us and showed us daily. He was never afraid to show his emotions around us. I think I respected and loved him for that more than anything else.

For I can do everything through Christ,

who gives me strength.

Philippians 4:13

stone 8

scarred seasons

For everything there is a season,
a time for every activity under heaven.
Ephesians 3:1

After the funeral I found it difficult to do the smallest of things. It was as if I couldn't wake up from a horrible nightmare. I felt like a dog circling round and round and round trying to find that perfect place to lay down. But there was no perfect place to lay down. Disbelief was all that existed for me. I was constantly on the verge of a panic attack type of feeling. EVERYTHING made me cry. A month or so before my dad went to Heaven I had gotten him hooked on watching Diagnosis Murder with me. It came on Thursday nights. We buried my dad's body on a Thursday. That night when I collapsed into my recliner I turned it on. The episode that night was the second part of a two part series. As it came on I fell to pieces as I realized my dad wouldn't get to see how it ended. I know this may sound unreasonable or even silly to some people, but as I said in the beginning of this book, there is no right or wrong way to feel.

Sleeping was a nightmare, but so was being awake. The week-ends were no different that the week-days. The weather didn't matter to me. Yes, I got up every morning and put one foot in front of the other. I got my husband off to work, took care of my girls, maintained the house, checked on mom and my brother, did the shopping, mowed my mom's yard every week, but I didn't feel alive. Every Monday and Tuesday the feeling of impending doom would wash over me. I would relive the last Monday that Dad was still here. All during the day I would think about the fact that my dad didn't have a clue it was going to be his last day. That made me so sad for some reason. Not that I would have wanted him to know, because that was one of the best days he'd had in a long time. I think it just brought me to such a state of reality I could hardly bear it. Every day I couldn't help but think that it could be "my" last day too. Mondays and Tuesdays were "dreadful days" for me for a very long time.

Pain was everywhere for me. Every time I rounded the corner to Mom and Dad's house, and for a split second thought Dad was home because his jeep was in the driveway, it would break my heart a little more. I remember falling to pieces in the meat department of my grocery store when I saw a T-bone steak. Yes, a T-bone steak. When was the last time you were comforted by the meat cutter in your grocery store? Memories swept over me of the old "T-bone Story" my dad used to tell about me when I was a little girl.

You see, when I was about three years old my mom and dad would take me to a local restaurant where we ate regularly. They were on a fairly tight budget at that time so they usually got the special and I got something from the child's menu.

Well, one time they were able to splurge a little and they got T-bone steak. They gave me bites and let me chew the meat from around the T-bone, which was the best part, and I loved it. My dad told me the "T" shaped bone was for my name, Tonya. My parents had no idea what they had created that day.

The next time we went in there to eat and the waitress asked us what we wanted I spoke up first and said, "I'd like a T-bone steak please." My mom, dad, and the waitress all looked at each other awkwardly, waiting for someone to say something. After a few silent seconds, my dad said, "You heard her, she said she'd like a T-bone steak please." When the waitress asked for my mom and dad's orders, they suddenly, weren't very hungry so they just ordered something small and some coffee. You see, that night they couldn't afford the T-bone steak and two other meals. I had no idea the sacrifice that took place during that meal, but I grew up to know all of the many sacrifices they made for everyone of us in the family, their entire lives.

After that day, there were many times my dad would

have me with him and would need to take care of business next door to the restaurant. So, he would walk me to the door and let me go into the restaurant by myself. I felt like such a big girl as I walked in and found the booth where I wanted to sit. Everyone that worked there treated me like I was their little girl and certainly looked out for me while I was there. My dad would stand at the window until they took my order. They would ask me what I wanted, and I would say, "I'd like a T-bone steak please." They would look at my dad and he would nod his head yes. I would sit there by myself and eat that T-bone steak until my dad would come and get me.

So, when I saw T-bone steak in the meat counter at my grocery store, I simply fell a part. Suddenly, my sweet memories of my life were causing me great pain.

I remember feeling as if my mouth was moving, but there was no sound coming out. It was like my body was moving from point A to point B, but I don't remember my feet moving. I knew I was going through the motions, but nothing had any meaning. I'm not saying I was the only one hurting. Every member of my family was traveling through their own personal nightmare.

Within a couple of weeks after my dad's death, my family had to make one of the toughest decisions we would ever have to make. We had to decide whether or not we would continue to do the show. This was the time of year when we were busy putting together our new show for the season. None of us could bear the thought of doing the show without dad. We each played such a huge part in our show and if one of us were missing it would leave a gigantic hole. So, we unanimously agreed to close our family show of 16 years. That was the second loss we had to endure that would forever affect each one of our lives.

As important as music had been to me all of my life, now, I couldn't even stand the thought of listening to the radio. I put away everything that reminded me of music. I put my piano away and got rid of my music books. I couldn't sing a note. I couldn't even stand to hear someone whistle. It just hurt my heart too much. Music always originated from my heart, but now there wasn't room in my heart for both music and pain. I had to wait until God planted that seed of music in my heart once again. Only then would it be able to grow, flourish, bear fruit, and eventually be harvested. For three and a half years my garden sat empty and bare. Eventually, God planted that seed.

There were so many difficult things we had to do during this time. A trip to the Social Security Office with my mom, getting the death certificates and getting my dad's name taken off everything in this world, except his tombstone. It made me so angry that every time I turned around someone else was taking his name off of something. It was as if they were erasing a little more of his memory each time they erased his name, making it like he had never existed at all. I understood the legal reasons why it had to be done, but it certainly didn't make it feel any better in my heart. No anger could possibly compare with the way I felt when I first laid eyes on his death certificate. My eyes immediately went to the box labeled "time of death." The time 7:57 a.m. will forever be imprinted on my heart. So, when I saw the time in that box marked as 7:00 a.m. I was livid. At 7:00 a.m. MY DAD WAS NOT DEAD! How dare they round-off the end of his life like that. Who did they think they were removing the last 57 minutes of his life as if it had no meaning, purpose, or importance. Maybe someone typing the certificate made a clerical error. Whatever the reason, I find it unimaginable that anyone could be so negligent with something so important.

Figuring out what to do with Dad's clothing and personal belongings was extremely difficult. So was having to move things from where Dad had last laid them. The place he laid his coat, the way he left a magazine by his chair or the cup he drank out of the last time. Finding little scraps of paper laying around with doodles on them or his handwriting on them made me cry. As difficult as all this was, I had to really watch myself so I didn't try to create a shrine of his things around me. I knew that wouldn't be healthy.

Everyone has their own way of coping. One is no better than the other. Some people may leave things unchanged for a long time, others may not be able to make changes fast enough. They may start moving furniture around, repainting their walls or changing their routines.

It is very common to want to keep items close to you

that belonged to your loved one. For me, it was my dad's fingernail clippers and a little coin holder he always carried his coins in. I got him a new one every Christmas and he had one all my life. It was always in his pocket with his fingernail clippers.

I don't care what anyone says, you just can't help but "what-if" yourself at least a little. You wouldn't be human if you didn't. You'll think of all the things you should have done or said. I allowed myself the right to feel these things because it's all part of the journey. If I just would have gone in the house when I dropped Chelsea off, I could have seen Dad one last time. Maybe I would have been there when he had his cardiac arrest and I could have started CPR immediately and maybe he would be alive today. See what I mean? You can't help but think of these things, but the key is not to obsess over them.

I found that after a while people around me acted as if the subject of my dad's death should be closed. For them it was done and over. For me it would never be over. How could I possibly "get over" something I was going to have to wake up with and go to sleep with every day for the rest of my life?

Four months down the road I found myself wishing someone, anyone, would say something to me about my dad. Maybe they didn't want to bring it up for fear of causing me pain or they didn't know what would be the right thing to say. I can't even express to you how it made me feel the first time

I went to my dad's grave and saw that someone besides our family had put flowers on it. They probably didn't even think that we would notice, but we did. It made me smile to know that someone else was thinking about him too. He was still alive in their heart like he was in mine. That was such a comforting thought for me.

People around me wanted me to act like my "old self," because the way I felt made them feel uncomfortable. Some wouldn't even ask me how I was doing if they passed me on the street. I think they were afraid I'd tell them. I think I felt lonlier months after my dad went to Heaven than when he first left.

Of course the "first" of everything was really lousy. Every holiday and special event that first year was awful. However, it wasn't just the holidays and special events that were affected for me. I even found, that as each new season came along, it brought with it a whole new reawakening of that deep sadness I first experienced those months ago. Yes, even the seasons carry scars now. Nothing has escaped the scars from my loss. I will see them in everything, and carry them with me forever.

With all the things I've had to deal with, I also know there will many more that lie ahead of me. No matter how much I would like my grief to end, it will never truly be over or finished for me. There is no "getting over it," I can only "get through it." My grief will always be as close to me as my next breath. Each and every day, for the rest of my life, there will always be something that will come along and trigger my grief, even if it's just for a moment in time. It may be a sight, a smell, a holiday, a sound, a laugh, a place, a thought, a meal, a song, a photograph, a dream, a memory...

For I can do everything through Christ,

who gives me strength.

Philippians 4:13

stone 9

the journey

See, I am sending an angel before you
to protect you on your journey and lead you safely
to the place I have prepared for you.
Exodus 23:20

I have decided that the word DYING only pertains to the person it's happening to. However, once the person takes their last breath and their heart beats its last beat, dying is then re-born to become a whole new creature. Dying then becomes death, and death is not about the person who has actually died. It's about the people left to continue the living. It's about a journey. A journey that started well before our lives began, and will continue long after our lives here have ended. This journey is like one long, continuous relay race. It's the reason we must continue to go forward when one of our loved one's journey here ends. If we don't continue the journey, we will be the one that dropped the baton in the relay race. Our loved one's journey would have been in vain. It would be incomplete. We are the next leg of their journey. A journey you may not have even been aware you were on, or maybe, only now see how important it has become in your life. It's all about the journey.

If you want to do something for someone, for goodness sake, do it while they're alive. My dad told me countless times that if someone hadn't come to see him in the last six months he darn sure didn't want them to come to his funeral. I get that now. I really get that now. So please call, visit, email or send a card to the people in your life that matter. Leave the past where it belongs if it has caused you to be separated from someone you love. Forgive and forget because that is exactly what God does for us. If we don't forgive others, God won't forgive us. There is no fight worth losing precious time with a loved one for. God does not promise us tomorrow, next week, or next year. He only promises us this very second in time. Don't waste that second fighting with your family. It can all be over in one single heartbeat. Trust me. Poof, gone in a second.

Once your loved one is gone, it is so important not to let anyone guilt you into doing things. Be prepared to hear things like, "You know that's not what your loved one would want you to do." They may be referring to the way you are grieving, a decision you made, something you were unable to do, or maybe something they want you to do. I remember hearing that phrase ring out like a church bell in a steeple.

In your own personal experience with death, you must also allow yourself freedom to be a little selfish sometimes. If you try to base your life on what others tell you your loved one would have wanted you to do, you will never gain any new ground on moving forward. Even though we face it daily on our journey, it's the new, untraveled path that is by far the most difficult.

People mean well. Some will tell you things like, "It will get better," "Time will heal all wounds," "Everything will be ok," and the infamous, "You know they're in a better place," (which I firmly believe). Now, to be polite I smiled and said yes, I know. All the while screaming at the top of my lungs on the inside that...NO, it won't be better, TIME can't even put a band-aid on it, EVERYTHING will never be ok again, and the fact that they are in a far better place only proves what I've said about death NOT being about the loved one that's gone. It's about us that are left behind. Just for the record, it was a lousy thing the day it happened. It's lousy right now, and it will be just as lousy the day my part of this journey ends. However, there is always a calm after every storm. I can't begin to express how deeply my gratitude runs for my precious Heavenly Father, for scooping me up in His loving arms and carrying me when I could no longer walk on my own.

This may sound very strange to some people, but I remember the day that I heard myself laugh for the first real time after my dad went to Heaven. I actually gasped and stopped laughing immediately. Why, you ask? It was in that very moment that I realized I was afraid of losing my grief completely. It was mine. It was the last thing I had that connected me to my dad. It was between him and me. Of course, I have my memories, but the grief was the last personal thing I shared with him. I was afraid if I lost my grief I would also lose my dad permanently. I knew I didn't want to live in deep sadness forever, but it had become almost a source of comfort for me. Yes, I know how twisted that sounds, but that was truly what I felt. I thought my grief was what was keeping my dad's memory alive for me. It took me a while to realize my dad's memory would always be alive in my heart.

I'm sure there are people that think my sadness will someday end completely. I would have to say that I disagree. My sadness may take on a new face, or come in a different color, or be felt to a different degree, but "gone" is something it will never be. Sure, I will laugh, smile, live, love, and be happy again. I do notice, however, after the loss of my dad the flowers seem slightly less brilliant. The sun seems a little less bright. The sounds of nature seem a little muffled.

I have come to realize that I will have to change so many things for the rest of my life. I will have to change our family and holiday traditions for the rest of my life. I will have to learn to set one less plate at our wonderful family dinners for the rest of my life. I will have to learn to buy one less birthday gift for the rest of my life. I will have to learn to live without my dad's hugs for the rest of my life. So THAT'S how I know my sadness will never truly be gone for the rest of my life. To have a loss this significant in my life is like losing every other beat of my heart.

For I can do everything through Christ,

who gives me strength.

Philippians 4:13

stone 10

one year later

New honors are constantly bestowed on me,
and my strength is continually renewed.
Job 29:20

∞ ∞ ∞

On the morning of January 12, 1999, I awoke feeling a little irritable. I really didn't want to talk much. I just wanted to be left alone with my thoughts. All day long I thought back to what Dad was doing on that day last year and what I was doing on that day. I still went through my daily routine. I cooked dinner and watched as the hands of the clock counted down what was Dad's last day a year ago.

All of a sudden I was back at Pizza Hut hearing that ambulance scream by and then the phone ringing. I began to cry. Every detail was being played out in my mind like a home movie. I'm not sure why, but I picked up the phone and called my brother. As we talked and I cried, the hands of the clock slowly moved past that horrible time when our world blew apart. I think I called him because I knew he would absolutely understand how I was feeling, even if I couldn't utter a single word.

I hung up the phone and sat down in the living room. The tears kept running down my cheeks as I tried to watch tv. I wasn't sobbing, the tears just flowed in a steady stream. Kevon was so wonderful. He always knew just what to say and when to not say anything at all. He knew how horrible this was and he was there for me all night as the time ticked away, one lonely second at a time. Even though we pretty much sat there in silence that night I always knew he was just a hug away.

As I put my head on my pillow that night there were still tears falling. I was desperately trying to drift off to sleep when suddenly it came back to me. "LIQUID LOVE." That's what the nurse in the hospital told us our tears were. Finally, a comfortng feeling washed over me and sleep finally came.

I didn't sleep well that night. I kept waking up and looking at the clock. Finally it was morning and I got Kevon's breakfast ready and saw him off to work. I realized I would be alone when 7:57 a.m. came. I fixed a cup of hot tea, sat down in the living room and waited. I had grown accustomed to waiting. As I watched the clock change from 7:56 a.m. to 7:57 a.m. I felt like I would explode. Then as quickly as that feeling came, it left. It just slipped away from me. I felt at peace. I walked over to a picture of my dad I had sitting on a table. The picture was of him having a great big laugh. I couldn't help but smile. One true gift he gave everyone he came in contact with was laughter. He gave it away freely. He certainly was the master of laughter.

Later that day I went to the cemetary. I didn't go all the time, but there were times I would go and just sit on the ground and trace the letters of his name on the headstone as I re-lived some of the wonderful memories of my life.

Everything was so beautiful at the cemetary that day. The night before we had some freezing rain and all the tree limbs and grass were covered in, what looked like, a sheet of glass. The grass crunched beneath my every step as I walked toward the grave. All the flowers on his grave looked like they were made of beautiful crystal china.

It was there I became very emotional. The reality seemed to set in all over again. For some strange reason it bothered me that day when I looked down at his headstone and found it was completely covered in ice. I couldn't see his name or anything else that was written on it. It looked like a gray block of ice. I went back to my car and got my windshield scraper to see if I could scrape it off. I worked and I worked but I couldn't get it off. I hated that it looked like a blank piece of stone laying there. I felt so lonely not being able to trace the letters of my father's name with my finger that day.

Now I can say I officially lived through the "first year" of an awful experience. On the first anniversary of my dad leaving me and going to Heaven, there were no awards given.

No confetti thrown. No bells rang out and there were no balloons waving in the air. No one called and I would just imagine only my immediate family even remembered what had happened a year ago on that day.

Anniversaries are something we usually look forward to. It marks a beautiful or wonderful event that we want to remember year after year to come. This was one anniversary I wasn't going to look forward to celebrating, year after year, for the rest of my life.

I spent that whole first year learning. I learned I wasn't literally going to "die" because I had lost my dad. It's just that living had now become more of a choice and a chore. Something that used to be as natural as breathing was now something I conciously chose to do. Finally, I came to a point where I wanted to find my way back to a place called happiness once again. Finally it was time.

Thinking back through my life, I think spring was Dad's favorite season. It didn't matter what month it was, he was ready for spring on the second day of January every year, even though it wasn't officially spring until March.

No matter what the calendar said, every year when he heard the first song of a whippoorwill he would tell me it was a sure sign of spring. Every year he would tell me that. He said some people thought their songs sounded sad and lonely. Not him though, it was something he looked forward to every year. Their song was such a symbol of new beginnings and wondrous re-births to him. In all the years, I never asked him why he felt that way about the whippoorwill's song, but it always made me smile.

The last spring of my dad's life he and I were standing at my garden's edge one evening when we heard a whippoorwill singing out in the woods. Once again he said, "When you hear a whippoorwill sing, it's a sure sign of spring." I smiled and said, "I know dad." Little did I know then, that would be the last time I would ever get to hear him tell me that. I can only imagine what the song of the whippoorwill must sound like where he's at now. I, on the other hand, will have to listen for their song, by myself, for the rest of my life.

The time finally came when I wanted to be able to look forward to things once again. I wanted to get to the point of where I could think of my dad without being consumed with immediate sadness. I wanted to be able to look at pictures of him without having tears run down my face. I wanted to be able to look forward to the seasons once again. I wanted a new beginning in my life. Maybe that's what the beginning of the second year would bring about for me.

For so long I felt like I was just stumbling along searching for something and never finding it. Finally, for the first time in a very long, sad year, I found myself looking forward to something. I could see the glimmer of a distant sunrise in the horizon of my life. Just as a sunrise marks the beginning of each new day, so would it be my new beginning. The time had come for me to listen. I had to walk quietly, yearn for life, live in love, and listen. I had to get very still and listen. I knew I had to be able to hear the whippoorwill's song with my heart and not just with my ears. After living through a year filled with nothing but questions, loss and sorrow, I was finally ready to listen. More than anything I wanted to be able to hear the whippoorwill sing again.

When that day came and the whippoorwill sang, echoing softly in the breeze, I could hear my dad say, "When you hear a whippoorwill sing, it's a sure sign of spring." I just smiled and said, "I know Dad."

For I can do everything through Christ,

who gives me strength.

Philippians 4:13

stone 11

the door

I know all the things you do, and I have opened a door for you that no one can close. You have little strength, yet you obeyed my word and did not deny me.
Revelation 3:8

The saying, "hindsight is 20/20," is so true. I had no idea that God was doing a huge work in me as I was living through the loss of my dad. I became a Born Again, Spirit-Filled, Kingdom Citizen, Christian when I was thirteen years old. I was raised in church and I went to a Christian College. I prayed and was involved in the churches I attended. I loved others and was always willing to help someone in need. I would have to say I was a "religious" person growing up. That's all we were taught. That's what filled the churches.

I was brought up in the era of the church that seemed to be more concerned with you following all of their man-made, denominational rules, than actually encouraging you to have your own RELATIONSHIP with Christ. I'm not faulting anyone, it was just the reality of church at that time. They wanted you in the buildings doing what they told you to do, but they never said anything about taking it out of the church and living it the other six days a week.

I believe the reason God began doing such a wonderful work within me during that year of my life, was because He knew I was going to need more strength, courage, and faith than I ever had before, to live through the next ten years of my life. I had no idea what was coming my way, but God did. Nothing catches Him by surprise.

It was at that point in my life I began to have a "RELATIONSHIP" with God, not just experience a "RELIGION." As with any relationship it takes effort and work on our part. Relationships are a two way street. My marriage would not have lasted for over 30 years if I had not worked at nurturing it, feeding it, building it, growing it and making it a priority in my life. That's exactly what I had to do to build a living, loving, continuous, and life changing relationship with God. I had to work at it.

All successful relationships are built on giving and taking, maintaining open lines of communication, putting the other person's needs before your own, and trust. You have to give to receive.

The first part of this book dealt more with the reality of death, what it meant to me, and how I came to terms with it as a "religious" person.

The second part of this book will also deal with a tremendous loss in my life. It won't be about me coming to terms with it this time, but having to live with the reality of losing someone so slowly, for so long, it was as if time stood still for almost ten years. The biggest difference for me this time was that I went through it while building an intimate and personal "relationship" with God.

I will share the overwhelming peace that I experienced while watching God take a horribly dark time in my life and turn it into something wonderful to Glorify His Name. I will share how I never let it steal my Joy and how I came to know that what satan meant for evil, God turned into something good. Most importantly, I want others to know that God is no respecter of person and what He did for me He will do for you.

I remember standing at my dad's bedside and thinking that I would never go through anything that bad ever again. Little did I know then, the door that was preparing to swing open in front of me. I wouldn't have a choice to walk through it or not. I would be shoved through it. I wouldn't have a choice of turning around and going back through the door to where I was before. I wouldn't have a choice of a lot of things for many years to come. Thank God, I didn't have a choice as to whether I would go through that door alone or not. God saw to that. I would never be alone for the rest of my life. It doesn't matter what kind of Goliath will ever stand in front of me, God will always see to it that I have a rock and a sling.

As I ventured into the second year after my dad went to

Heaven, I knew something would have to change for me to be able to begin living again. It was then that I realized for us to truly be able to begin living our lives again we would have to move away, and so our journey began.

For I can do everything through Christ,
who gives me strength.
Philippians 4:13

stone 12

the plan

For I know the plans I have for you, says the Lord.
They are plans for good and not for disaster,
to give you a future and a hope.
Jeremiah 29:11

∞ ∞ ∞

I'm not sure of the exact day or time it became a member of my family. I do know that by the time it made itself known, it had already been with us for several years. I don't remember the exact moment things turned from being something I could easily explain away, to the crushing reality there was an unwelcome stranger, intruding itself into my family. I just remember the moment I realized how much I despised this horrible thing that had forced itself into our lives.

The death of my father is what escalated things. Sure, there were little things we noticed the whole last year of our show and my dad's life. Maybe even before that. They were so subtle in the beginning we could easily explain them away as stress, having a lot on her mind or just not concentrating.

It was after my dad's death that the presence of this beast finally reared its ugly head and showed itself to us. We could no longer explain it away as "normal" for anyone's life. Looking back, I realize I probably ignored it for quite some time. I wasn't intentionally ignoring it, I just couldn't see it clearly enough to name it. I ignored it until one day it hit me right between the eyes. Then I could ignore it no more.

My brother and his family moved first and then my family did. Our oldest daughter stayed with my mom when we left so she wouldn't be alone. After my mom's house sold, "The Plan" was for her to come and live with us until she found her a place, then she could get a start at a new life too.

We really began working on getting our lives back to some form of normal. Even though it was going to have to be a "NEW" normal. We all really dug in and worked hard.

It was a devastating day when I realized "The Plan" would never come to be. We would never see "The Plan" come to life. What a tremendous set back for us in trying to find our "NEW" normal.

That's when I found out the hard way that OUR plans are not what matters. OUR plans aren't always according to God's purpose for our lives. We have to know when to "Let Go, and Let God take care of us." He knows what's best for us in every situation.

You can make many plans,
but the Lord's Purpose will prevail.
Proverbs 19:21

I also stopped planning for the future and began living in the very moment I was in each and every day. I remember telling my husband one day that I couldn't stand to talk about next year or the next five years. It was simply too difficult. It made me feel like I could only gain false hope looking to the future. I only saw black in front of me. The future was not mine to plan for anymore. Sometimes I wasn't even sure how to get through the next hour. There were no more vacations for many, many years. No week-end trips. No spontaneous get-a-ways. Every day was just like the day before. My husband used to say every day was "Groundhog Day" for us. We lived the same thing every single day. Then the alarm would go off then next morning and we'd get up and walk the same footsteps as the day before. We couldn't make any new footprints. We came to realize that if we didn't get it exactly right yesterday, we would get another chance to do it all over again the next day. How true that was.

I found myself beginning to lean more and more on God and I felt him guiding more and more of my footsteps. I still had no idea of what lay before me. How could I, it was unimaginable. I think it was a blessing from God that I didn't know what the next 10 years of my life were going to be like. I'm not sure I could have focused on what I needed to do today, for dreading tomorrow, the next day, the next week, the next month, and the next year. Conquering one minute was something I believed I could do. I didn't think that would be too overwhelming for me. Conquering more than that was not something I was able to wrap my mind around.

My relationship with God was beginning to grow and become alive for me in my every day life. It wasn't just in "church" that I thought about God, praised God or talked to God. We began to have conversations in the kitchen, on the porch, while I was doing the laundry and while I was taking care of my mom. I didn't have to be sitting in a "pew" in a building with a "steeple" on top of it to be close to God. He truly came ALIVE for me. Probably for the first time, I really KNEW He was with me, ALL THE TIME.

"The Plan" that we had looked forward to was not to be. At least not the way we had dreamed it to be. She did sell her house. We did go and load up her belongings in a truck. We did bring her to live with us. That's as far as we ever got with "The Plan."

For I can do everything through Christ,

who gives me strength.

Philippians 4:13

stone 13

old roads became new

For soon I must go down that road
from which I will never return.
Job 16:22

Just like the loss of my dad escalated the symptoms, so did my mom moving in with us. Within a month of her moving in with us I was sick with concern of what was wrong with my precious mother. What was happening to the mom that would sit in the yard with me as a young girl and make dresses out of leaves, for dolls made out of sticks? What was happening to the mom that used to let me stand up in a chair to help her roll out dumplings, and never complained about the mess I made with the flour? What was happening to the mom that would lie down in bed with me at night and take me on a wonderful adventure with just her words and imagination? What was happeing to the mom that did all those same things with her grandchildren? What was happening to my mom?

One of the first things I noticed when she moved in with us was she seemed confused and overwhelmed with balancing her bank statement and even keeping the register of her checkbook in order. Both were completely out of character for her. She ran three businesses with one hand tied behind her back for years. At first, the bank statement didn't seem out of the ordinary to me, because the statements were different than the ones she was familiar with from her previous bank. Since we had lived there for five months before she got there, I simply offered to help her with them. I didn't really notice for a while, but little by little, she wasn't having me "help" her, she was turning them over to me to do them for her. Every month when her bank statement came she would quietly put it on my desk and never say a word. Then I would balance her bank statement for her, quietly put it back on her desk and never say a word. One thing I came to know about this hideous disease was that it wasn't always what WAS said, but what WASN'T said that screamed the loudest and told the most.

I will never forget the day my walls came crashing down and I knew I had to do something. Mom had lived with us for one month. It was my birthday, I was at home, sitting as still as possible in a recliner, in horrible pain from shingles. It was on the back of my neck and the pain ran all the way up to the top of my head. It hurt to breathe. It even hurt to blink my eyes.

My mother wanted to go to Walmart to buy a blouse so I went with her. When we got home I went straight back to the recliner and my mom went to her room. About thirty minutes after we got home she came running into the living room almost in tears. She had her Walmart receipt in one hand and her checkbook in the other. I asked her what was wrong. She told me she had bought a blouse, paid cash for it, but now she couldn't figure out how to put it in her checkbook register. There was such a desperation in her voice it broke my heart. She was frantic. I was STUNNED, but I didn't want to upset her anymore than she already was. I calmly explained that she had paid cash for it and wouldn't need to put it in her checkbook unless she wrote a check. I tried to be as calm as possible and make light of it. I told her I had done the same thing before, hoping it would calm her down. She had a peculiar look in her eyes that day. One I had never seen before. One I would never forget. It was a look of fear, bewilderment, and anger all rolled into one. She grabbed two handfuls of her hair and started shaking and crying. I asked her what was wrong and she said, "I just want to put on a pair of boots and walk out of this life." She had never said anything like that before. In one way it sounded silly and odd, and didn't really make any sense. In another way it was exactly what she was wishing she could do.

I comforted her and calmed her down all the while I was screaming at the top of my lungs inside my head. A couple of minutes later she went back to her room and nothing was ever said about it again. For her, it was as if it had never happened, but NOT for me. I would never be able to forget that look in her eyes, ever.

I began to notice that even though I took the same route to the store she couldn't seem to remember how to get there. I would ask her to tell me how to get to the store as I was driving and she would try but I could tell she really didn't have a clue. Then one day as we were driving to the same store we'd driven to time and time again, she began to look around with a child-like enthusiasm and said, "Well, I've never been on this road before." I couldn't even speak. I went numb. I wanted to open the car door and jump out of the car while it was moving. At that moment, all I could hear was my heart pounding in my ears. I desperately hoped she was joking with me because I couldn't belieive she had said something like that. IT WAS NO JOKE. Nothing about this was a JOKE. If it was, it was a SICK, SICK JOKE.

Trust in the Lord with all your heart,
do not depend on your own understanding.
Proverbs 3:5

Deep down in my heart I knew what was wrong with her before I even took her to the doctor, but I had to be sure. The only way I could think of to get her to go to the doctor, was to tell her she needed to get set up with a new doctor since she'd just moved there. So I secretly wrote a letter to the doctor describing my mom's actions and symptoms over that past years and took the letter to him a week before her appointment. If it was what I suspected, I didn't want her to be told that monstrous word. I didn't want that word ringing in her head for the rest of her life. So I told the doctor if he could guarantee me that she would benefit from being told, then I would be the one to tell her myself. But, if she wouldn't benefit from knowing, then I didn't want her to ever be told. After all, I already knew what it was and I believe she already knew what it was too.

There were multiple tests done that day to rule out the possibility that any other problem could be causing her symptoms. For me, the most heart-breaking part of the visit was when the doctor gave her a test by asking her questions. With each question she would look at me with such a desperate, pitiful, pathetic look in her eyes, pleading with me to give her the answer. The doctor asked her if she noticed that she kept looking at me for the answers. She looked at him as if she wanted to cry and kick him in the shins all at the same time. I wanted to run out of the room and just keep on running, but I looked out the window instead and ignored her looks until the test was over. I never hated myself more than I did at that very moment for having to do that to her. I felt sick to my stomach. I wanted to punch a pillow. More than hating myself though, I hated this "thing" that was infiltrating my family. I felt like I was abondoning her when she needed me more than she'd ever needed me before, but we had to know the truth. The ugly, dispicable, ruthless, cowardly truth. So all I could do was look out the window, choke back my tears and pray. Pray that she would be able to forgive me for not helping her when she needed me most. Pray that I could forgive myself.

And you will know the truth,
and the truth will set you free.
John 8:32

As I sat in the doctor's office, biting my cheek and trying not to cry or scream, I felt our roles of mother and daughter reversing as I sat there glaring out the window, and it made me physically ill. The whole time we were there I was praying they would find out whatever she had was something that could easily be treated. After all, she was only in her fifties and was very healthy. I realize now that I was in denial. A few days later, when the doctor called me with the results of all her tests, I hung up the phone and knew denial was a luxury I would no longer be able to have in my life. Once I heard the words, "Early Onset Alzheimer's Disease," denial immediately became a thing that would only live in my past from that day forward. I knew this was something I would have to meet head on. How could I possibly have known that it would feel like I was running headlong into a freight train?

That was a very dark day for me. Thinking back, I think it was God's way of letting me feel a mere fraction of the helplessness my mother would be forced to feel the rest of her life here on earth. It was His way of nuturing the growth of my compassion. The compassion that I was going to need to feel for my mother's situation for a very long time.

I saw and felt God's Grace and Mercy raining down on me when my husband came home that evening and asked what the doctor had said. With my heart breaking and tears rolling down my face I told him the doctor said it was Early Onset Alzheimer's Disease and I didn't know what we were going to do. He said, "Well, we'll just take care of her." I wasn't surprised that he said that, because that's the kind of relationship he had always had with my mom and dad. Then I told him I needed for him to understand something. I told him this could be the next twenty years of our lives. I'll never forget the next moment as long as I live. I believe it forever defined the next nine and a half years of our lives. Without even taking a breath and with tears streaming down his face he said, "I don't care if it's the next thirty years." At that moment, I didn't know what our future was going to hold. I didn't know how earth shatteringly difficult the next nine and a half years were actually going to be. I didn't know what kind of toll it would have on us personally, emotionally, financially or spiritually. What I did know at that very moment, however, was that WE would be ok. I knew we wouldn't have to go through it alone, and whatever strength we would need, our Precious God would provide it for us.

It was after that day, that I remember getting up each morning and standing firm on Philippians 4:13. I did that day after day, month after month, year after year. I knew I would need the greatest strength possible to conquer all that would come my way every day. That kind of strength could only come from my Lord. Every morning I started my day saying that verse as I got out of bed and headed for the shower. It was only because I had actively been pursuing a living "RELATIONSHIP" with my Heavenly Father, that I was actually able to believe it. That verse didn't make the disease any less horrible to live with, the length of the days any shorter, the reality of my mother's life any easier to understand or the heartbreak I experienced every second any less. What it did do, was give me the peace of knowing I COULD DO EVERYTHING THROUGH CHRIST WHO GIVES ME STRENGTH.

For I can do everything through Christ,

who gives me strength.

Philippians 4:13

stone 14

the why revealed

Because of God's tender mercy, the morning light from heaven is about to break upon us, to give light to those who sit in darkness and in the shadow of death, and to guide us to the path of peace.
Luke 1:78-80

≡∞≡ ≡∞≡ ≡∞≡

I don't think we would have been human if the word "WHY" wouldn't have entered our minds, because it did. I know we wondered why, that right on the heels of losing our dad and our family business, we were also faced with losing our mom. We were so busy dealing with the reality of our situation, however, that we just didn't allow ourselves to dwell on the "WHY." We knew nothing beneficial would come if we allowed ourselves to get stuck on the dead-end street of "WHY." Even if God could have sent me down a hand-written note telling me the good that was going to come out of this and why it was happening, would it really have made me feel any better in the moment? No. My mom and dad's lives were still the payment for the good God would bring out of it. We knew what lay before us and simply chose to persevere. After all, we didn't really have a choice. One thing my mom always taught me was, if life gives you lemons, then make lemonade. Before this journey was to be over, I would become the best lemonade maker ever.

Looking back, my brother and I realized that there were symptoms beginning at least five years before our mother was diagnosed with Alzheimer's. We were so engulfed with our own horrible grief from losing our dad, that the two years following his death were nothing but a blur for us. I thought some of her odd behavior was because of her grief. After all, she had lost her husband of forty two years. I knew how I felt, and thought she had to be feeling just as bad as I was. I can see now that symptoms were certainly there, but we were all doing good just to get up each morning and put one foot in front of the other until it was time to lay our heads down on our pillows each night. How could we have known that this would be how our mother's life was going to end? How could we have known that this disgusting disease would come to live with us for more than fifteen years? No, that's not correct. How could we have known that this disgusting disease would come to live with us for the rest of our lives? How could we have possibly known that the disease of Alzheimer's would not just affect our mother's life but it would affect our lives forever. It went away for our mom, but it will never go away for us as long as we're on this earth.

One morning, a few months after mom's diagnosis, I woke up after having a dream, with a peace bubbling up inside of me that I hadn't felt for a very long time. I finally knew WHY my dad had to go to Heaven when he did.

A couple of days later I called my brother to tell him about my dream. As I started to talk he told me he had a dream just a couple of nights before too and that he knew WHY dad had to go to Heaven when he did. I couldn't believe it. I wasn't prepared for what he told me.

As he began to share his dream with me all I could do was cry. We both started talking at the same time as we shared our dreams with each other. I was shocked when I realized that on the exact same night, living three and a half hours apart, we both had the exact same dream. We both saw our parents sitting on their couch and saw the brokenness and anger in our father's eyes as he was trying to deal with the horrible disease that was consuming his precious wife of forty two years.

At that moment we were actually happy and relieved that he did not have to endure this paralyzing nightmare and watch his wife die such a long and horrific death. We were more than willing to do it for him. I like to think of it as the greatest and final gift we were ever able to give our father. A gift freely given with hearts full of unconditional love. He would have laid down his life for any of us. This was the least we could do for him.

In peace I will lie down and sleep,
for you alone, O Lord, will keep me safe.
Psalm 4:8

As my brother and I talked that day, a type of closure took place for us and a peculiar type of peace entered our hearts that bonded us together for the journey that lay before us. I'm not saying we were happy to have lost our dad or with the thought of losing our mom, but after two and a half years we finally knew WHY both things happened the way they did. I think feeling God's Grace at that very moment is what gave me the courage and determination to endure what each day was going to bring, and feel confident that I would be victorious over anything that satan would try to throw at me. I firmly believe that God will never take me to, what He won't take me through. Now I try to make it a point every day to thank Him for that very fact.

God never promised we wouldn't have to go through storms in our lives. What He does promise is to hold our hand as we walk into the storm. To pick us up and carry us during the worst part of the storm, and to lead us out on the other side of the storm. He has shown me time and time again, that I WILL walk out of it better than I was when I walked into it, and each time my relationship with Him grows stronger for what we went through together. Every single time.

On the day my father went to Heaven, I knew my life

would forever be changed and NOTHING would ever be normal again. I was absolutely right. Then, just as we were starting over and trying to find a "new" normal, we got the rug pulled out from under our feet again with my mom's diagnosis of Alzheimer's. So, once again, we did the only thing we could do. Once again we started over. Once again we dug in. Would it be the last time we would have to start over? No. We set out trying to find, yet another, "new" normal. We all locked arms and hearts and headed for the battlefield, once again.

I've come to believe that my life will continuously be in one phase or another of starting over to find "new" normals for as long as I live. Our lives are steadily evolving toward the destiny God created for each one of us. Our lives are constantly changing, and will forever. If they didn't, we'd become like a stagnant pond. We are all just works in progress. We are simple lumps of clay tossed onto the potter's wheel. Those potter's hands belong to God. Sometimes I feel like I'm a hamster on a giant wheel running and I can't get off of it. I'm just running and running and running and running...

For I can do everything through Christ,

who gives me strength.

Philippians 4:13

stone 15

until there are none

Laughter can conceal a heavy heart,
but when the laughter ends, the grief remains.
Proverbs 14:13

As I settled into another "new" normal after my mom's diagnosis, I began to find it impossible NOT to notice the changes that had already taken place in her. Even though I wanted to ignore the differences, I couldn't. It was like trying to ignore my reflection in a mirror. Even if I didn't look at my reflection, I knew it was still there.

I found it surprising that the things that truly upset me in the beginning didn't seem to bother me after a day, a week, a month, or a year passed by. I think it was because all of the things that I had to learn to cope with in the beginning were being replaced with a whole new set of things for me to cope with continuously. It seemed with every heartbeat new things were being lost. With every heartbeat my mom was forever slipping further away from me. With every heartbeat she was dying just a little bit more. With every heartbeat she was fading away from my life.

In the beginning, it would upset me for her to ask me fifteen times a day what day it was, or to ask me nine times every day what time my husband would get home from work. In no time at all, I didn't even blink when she would ask me those things, but I would lose my breath when she would catch me off guard with a new question she had never asked me before. I think it was because every time she would ask me a new question or lose another ability or function, it caused me to have to admit all over again that she had Alzheimer's. Or maybe I should say, that Alzheimer's had her. Certainly no one would chose to have that dreaded disease if they had a choice.

When she was first diagnosed, I was surprised to find myself experiencing grief. I wondered how I could be grieving the loss of my mother when she was still here with me. It wasn't long before I began to notice that this grief was different than the grief I experienced after losing my dad. With my dad, I was able to find my way through each stage and eventually move through them to the end. I've never stopped grieving his loss completely, even after years, but now it just comes in subtle waves. With my mom, I could never get through all the stages because every time I blinked my eyes she lost another memory, function, or ability and my grief would begin all over again. She was still right there in front of me, I could reach out and touch her, but she was drifting away from me like a lost ship at sea, disappearing off into the night's thick fog.

I found myself living in a state of, what I called, "perpetual grief." Never getting through the stages before they would begin again, over and over and over this continued to happen. It was the never ending grief. It was like an involuntary reflex. Stopping the perpetual grief would have been like trying to stop my heart from beating, or stop my blood from flowing.

When every second of your every day is filled with perpetual grief it can swallow you alive if you're not careful. When you eat it, drink it, sleep it, and breathe it, the grief can consume you if let your guard down. That was my greatest battle to fight. I was determined my grief was not going to consume me, but it was the most difficult thing I've ever done. I could never put it down or set it aside because it would once again pump through my veins with every loss my mother endured.

This was no short battle. This was no easy battle. It was my battle, however, to fight. It raged on for more than fifteen years. I had to make a conscious choice every single morning to NOT let it steal my JOY. So, with the strength only God could give me, a prayer in my heart and a song on my lips, I put on the full armor of God and climbed out of bed each day. Then I would rush, hand in hand with God, to the front line to storm the enemy.

The eternal God is your refuge,
and his everlasting arms are under you.
He drives out the enemy before you; he cries out, "Destroy them!"
Deuteronomy 33:27

Above all else, in my Caregiving experience, I came to know that Alzheimer's is a very cruel disease. It robs you of your memories, one by one, until there are none. It does it slowly and steadily, without any rhyme or reason. It's very methodical in the stripping away of your memories, and it doesn't stop until you are like a tree in the winter that's been stripped bare of its leaves. You never know which memory will be the next one Alzheimer's chooses to take. You can't pick or choose which memory you are willing to release to the disease, or at what time. The disease calls all the shots. You have no choice or say so in the matter at all. I would say that's cruel, wouldn't you?

Our memories are so precious and personal to us. Sometimes they're all we have left of something or someone that was wonderful from our past. I feel like our memories identify us, just as individually and precisely, as our fingerprints do. There are no two people who have the exact same fingerprints and no two people who have the exact same memories. So, as Alzheimer's deliberately and systematically robs people of their memories, it also slowly robs them of who they were, who they are, and who they would have become. It robs them of their individual identity.

It forces them to grieve the loss of themselves for years and years. I would say that's cruel, wouldn't you?

Alzheimer's steals every memory from them that they've ever made in their entire life, and prevents them from ever creating another new memory for the rest of their life. I would say that's cruel, wouldn't you?

Alzheimer's forces them into a world of silent darkness, even with their eyes wide open. They slip away further and further into a midnight abyss that they can never return from. The sparkle in their eyes fades into a dull, gray blankness. I would say that's cruel wouldn't you?

Their bodies turn against them as the disease sucks their life right out of them. Their muscles turn to jelly as they can no longer walk or stand, and their organs begin to slowly fail. I would say that's cruel, wouldn't you?

Their once ample vocabulary is taken from them and transformed into grunts, sounds and eventually empty silence. I would say that's cruel, wouldn't you?

I think the definition of Alzheimer's Disease should be listed in the dictionary like this: Alzheimer's Disease - CRUEL.

For I can do everything through Christ,

who gives me strength.

Philippians 4:13

stone 16

dreading the nights

My wound is severe, and my grief is great.
My sickness is incurable, but I must bear it.
Jeremiah 10:19

Since we chose not to tell my mom that she had Alzheimer's, I was determined that her life would be as normal as the disease would allow. I was determined that love would continue to be the basis on which I would make every decision concerning her care, every single day, for the rest of her life. As long as there was breath in my body, I was not going to allow this evil disease to rob her of her dignity, along with her memories and eventually her life. Alzheimer's would not take her dignity.

That's not to say, that our lives were all "cotton candy" and "rainbows." In fact, that would be the furthest thing from the truth. I came to know in my long, difficult journey that it's not always what you're given to deal with that's important, but it's the way you choose to deal with it that can make all the difference in the world.

So many changes had already begun to surface by the time we got the diagnosis. There was the morning she went in the bathroom to take a shower, just like she had done every morning. I met her coming out of the bathroom just minutes after she had gone in. I noticed a very troubled and scared look on her face and asked her what was wrong. With tear-filled eyes she looked at me and said, "I don't know what to do. I don't know how to take a shower. Will you come in the bathroom with me and help me?" Even though it completely shook me to my inner core, I didn't want to make her feel any more scared than what I saw in her eyes, so I told her no problem and between the two of us we'd figure it out. I smiled at her reassuringly and gave her a hug. Then I proceeded to follow her into the bathroom, stand outside the shower and coach her through her entire shower, step by step, as I wiped away the tears.

That didn't happen everyday after that. Some days she could do it and some days she couldn't. Eventually she was no longer able to even know what a shower was, much less be able to take one by herself. That shows you how sneaky Alzheimer's can be. One day it takes away, then tricks you into thinking it's giving it back, only to take it away forever.

We began to notice that the evenings were especially unsettling for my mom, just as it was for us having to watch her go through them. She had already begun to pace throughout the house all day long, but in the evenings she would get more agitated with the pacing. She would pace from room to room, from window to window and from door to door trying to get out of the house.

We would try to have her sit with us in the living room to watch a movie and she would sit for maybe three minutes and then jump up and start to pace like a tiger in a cage. I would sit her back down and cover her up. Just as I would sit back down she would already be folding up the blanket and would get up again and start pacing. This happened thirty or more times every evening.

If we wanted to watch a movie, my husband would stand at one door and I would stand at the other as we watched our movie and would let her pace all she wanted, because at least we knew she couldn't get out of the house with us standing in front of the doors.

I learned that this exasperating, evening phenomena that came to live in my home every evening, was called "Sundowning Syndrome."

The term "sundowning" describes a state of confusion in a person that is especially noticable at the end of the day and into the night. Sundowning is a symptom, not a disease, that occurs in people with Alzheimer's disease.

No one really knows why it happens, we just know it happens. It may have something to do with the fact they become more tired at the end of the day. It could be their internal "body clock" confuses the night with the day. Maybe it's because they start having delusions, and the delusions prevent them from knowing the difference between dreams and reality. Combine all of that with the fact they require less sleep as they age and there you have the recipe for "Sundowning."

So we began to close the blinds every day before the sun went down so she couldn't see it getting dark. I began turning on lights in the house before it got dark. I put a night light in her bedroom so she wouldn't be in the complete darkness. I don't know how much all of that actually helped, but at least I felt like I was doing something for her.

She didn't sleep well at all during the nights, therefore, we didn't either. We kept our bedroom door open at all times so we could hear her if she started down the hall. We'd jump up and lead her back to bed. Sometimes we'd do that as many as fifteen or more times every night.

She never could tell me why she kept getting up or where she was wanting to go. Each time she would get up, it was as if it were the first time for her. She had no idea she had already gotten up nine times before. Night after night, I would just pray for God to protect her through the night.

There came a time when I slept in the bed with her and my husband slept on the floor outside her bedroom door. That way if she didn't wake me up when she slipped out of bed, she would wake him up when she tried to go through her bedroom door.

In all the years she lived with us and we took care of

her, she never escaped from our home or got lost one time. Looking back, I know that was God's Grace shining down on us.

The Lord is my rock, my fortress, and my savior;
my God is my rock, in whom I find protection.
He is my shield, the power that saves me,
and my place of safety.
Psalm 18:2

Along with her mental decline, during this stage of her Alzheimer's also came Obsessive Compulsive Behaviors. She would go in the bathroom or kitchen and open and close every drawer and door over and over and over again, all hours of the day or night. She wouldn't stop until one of us went in and stopped her. She could never tell me why she was doing it. She would brush her teeth for minutes on end until we would have to stop her. She would fold and unfold clothes repeatedly. She would wash off the kitchen counters until I thought she would wear the color off of my dishcloths.

One day she wanted to go out and wash her new car that she was so proud of. I watched out the kitchen window as she washed her car for almost 3 hours. She wouldn't stop. She would get all the way around the car and then she would go around it again and again for hours. Finally, when I was about to scream because I couldn't take it anymore, I asked Kevon if he would please go out and make her stop.

Seeing her do things like that, is what made that stinking disease so very real to me. It was as if it was taunting me or laughing in my face.

She became obsessed with her hair. She would get it cut or highlighted and go back to have it done again in just a couple of weeks. I would go to the Salon and talk to the stylist when mom wasn't there so she would understand. I hated always feeling like I was running interference for that mind-robbing disease.

I began to notice that she was losing words. Just randomly losing words. She would begin to speak and in the middle of a sentence she couldn't think of the word that came next. Then she would get flustered and embarrassed. I never made an issue out of it at all. I would either try to help her by gently saying the word or just allow her to casually change the subject. Two specific examples of her losing a word have never left my mind and probably never will. In fact, they've actually become precious memories that we've passed on through families and friends to be remembered forever.

One day, as my mom and I were sitting on the front porch, a bright red Cardinal landed out in the yard in front of us. Just as we both noticed it my mom said, "Oh my, what a beautiful..............," and then there was that awkward silence that took over for a minute or so, as she searched for the word "Cardinal." All of a sudden, shattering the silence she said, "What a beautiful Little Red Coat." For a second I thought, Little Red Coat? Then it made perfect sense to me. It was the closest thing she could come up with that described what she was seeing. It did look like a bird with a little red coat on. To this day I still feed birds in my backyard, and still call those bright red birds, "Little Red Coats."

The other moment I remember, I was looking out our huge picture window one winter morning to see the first snow of the season gently falling to the ground. Ever since I was a child, my mom and I would get excited when the first snow began to fall. So I yelled for her to come and look. As she ran into the room and looked out, she reminded me of a little girl gazing out the window, with glistening eyes, as she admired the beauty. Then very excitedly she said, "Oh look, it's..............," silence fell in the room once again as she struggled to find the word "snowing." After what seemed like hours she finally said, "Oh look, it's soft-falling." In her mind she couldn't remember the word "snowing," so she called it what she was actually seeing out the window. She saw white "soft-falling" flakes. So, for the rest of my life, when white blankets the ground in the winter, it will forever be called "Soft-Falling." It was just such a beautiful word picture to me. I don't think I will ever say it and not smile.

It was so unbelievably sad, that the loss of her vocabulary had to become something that routinely continued to happen, until one day it was no longer there at all. It was just gone. Where did it go? How could it have just disappeared? Or was she being held as a silent prisoner? Able to think, hear and understand, but unable to communicate with us at all in the end. Those are just some of the questions that would ring in my head daily.

I cared for my mother and was forced to watch this disgusting disease ravage her mind and body. I always had questions, but no one could really give me any answers.

No one handed me a "How-To Manual" when my mom was diagnosed with Alzheimer's. They handed me a prescription for Aricept and told me it might give her six more months. They gave me a couple of prescriptions to help calm her irritability and anxiousness and sent me on my way.

Soon, I figured out why they didn't give me a manual. It was because there was NO "How-To Manual" for this disease. No one has it figured out. I learned along the way that if you meet one person with Alzheimer's, then you've met one person with Alzheimer's. No two people will have exactly the same symptoms. No two people will act the same way.

No one has the answers as to how to cope and battle this disease. There is no cure. There is no treatment. There are no real answers. We had to find our own way on this journey one step at a time. We had to figure out what would work for my mom each step of the way. If something didn't work, we just kept trying until we found something that did.

We did that day after day, for nine and a half years. I was always having to come up with NEW ways to solve the same problems, because one day it would work and the next day it wouldn't work.

I felt like I was putting together a giant jigsaw puzzle over and over and over again. But each time I put it together there were more and more pieces missing. I didn't know they were missing until I had worked so hard putting it all together. All that work, only to find out I would never get to see the whole picture of the puzzle ever again.

For I can do everything through Christ,

who gives me strength.

Philippians 4:13

stone 17

loss and changes

But the jar he was working on did not turn out as he hoped, so he crushed it into a lump of clay again and started over.
Jeremiah 18:4

∞ ∞ ∞

By this time, my mother had certainly moved into the moderate stage of the disease. Moderate.....I'm not sure I can say there's anything "Moderate" about Alzhiemer's. It was so heartbreaking to have to watch her spin out of control at times with irritableness, agitataion and frustration. Not that I didn't understand it or even feel like she deserved to feel those things, but it was still heartbreaking to watch. She absolutely had a right to be angry, furious, enraged, and irate. I know I was.

On one of her early doctor visits it was recommended that I attend a support group meeting. I had never been to any kind of support group before in my life, but I found one in our town and my husband and I went.

I can't express the type of "reality check" I experienced when I walked into the room. Not only were we the youngest people in the room, but every single person at the meeting was older than my mom, by at least ten to fifteen years. That's when I realized just how much worse it was because she was only in her fifties. All of these people were there talking about their parents with Alzheimer's, but their parents were in their eighties or nineties.

I sat quietly during the meeting. The person leading the meeting told me I immediately needed to go to an attorney and be appointed my mother's Durable Power of Attorney, get her a living will, and a will drawn up. I was so concerned with how I was going to get this done without mom becoming alarmed or overly curious. How was I going to get her to an attorney. When I look back at those times, I felt God's arms of love and compassion wrapped around me.

I waited for a couple of days so I could build up my courage. Then I started a conversation with her about her will needing to be changed since dad had passed away. I just eased into the fact she may need someone appointed to make decisions for her IF she were ever unable to. She almost looked relieved. She asked me to make the appointment and we got it all taken care of. So, the thing I was most concerned about was simply erased. She didn't ask any questions or get defensive. Again, it was absolutely God's Grace. He always told me I would never be alone. I can't describe the peace that was living in me now.

For the Lord your God is a merciful God;
he will not abandon you or destroy you or forget the solemn covenant he made with your ancestors.
Deuteronomy 4:31

It amazed me to watch how the disease progressed. It was like having your foot on the accelerator of a car. At times the disease progressed like you had pushed the accelerator all the way to the floor. Other times, it was as if you had taken your foot off of the accelerator and was coasting. Either way, it always progressed. There was always loss and change taking place no matter what.

This will give you a slight idea of the affects the disease had on my mother during the first three and a half years after her diagnosis. This is a very short list compared to what actually took place.

SHE COULD NO LONGER:

- Balance her bank statements.
- Write checks or balance her checkbook.
- Use cash or a credit card.
- Learn her phone number or address.
- Find her way around our town.
- Work the door locks or window buttons in her car.
- Remember our birth dates or her own, at times.

- Name the next holiday coming up.
- Remember how to use the microwave each time.
- Remember how to turn on the oven.
- Follow a recipe.
- Remember what she ate or when she ate.
- Remember our names all the time.
- Remember the answers to questions she asked.
- Make decisions or choices, big or small.
- Carry on logical or rational conversations.
- Do her own hair or apply make-up.
- Read or comprehend things read to her.
- Cook.
- Shop.
- Drive her car.

This list was always growing and never ending. So were the losses and changes all of us had to sit back and helplessly watch happen to her. No one can tell me this disease did not come straight from the pits of satan's hell. Only someone as evil, malicious, and despicable as satan could do that.

It was also during this time that my mother started having delusions and hallucinations. I remember going into her room one night to get her all tucked into bed. As I got her to lay down, she kept looking over to the left in her room. She had such a pleasant look on her face and was nodding and smiling and waving in that same direction. I asked her what she was doing and she said, "I've been playing with those little girls and I want to wave goodbye to them." The saddest thing about what she told me was that it didn't phase me one bit. Those type of things I heard frequently now.

There were many times if she heard a dog bark, doorbell ring, a horn blow or someone ask a question on TV, she thought it was acutally happening in real life. She would talk to the TV and answer questions as if those people were standing in her room. At times she even argued with the TV.

There were so many times she would lift one of her hands straight up towards the sky as if someone were reaching out to her to take hold of her hand. This happened a lot during the last month of her life. She would look up and move her mouth like she was talking. She would always smile so sweetly as she reached her hand up; it made me cry.

Those were the kind of things that happened during my long journey that I started calling, "My Little Hugs From God." Moments that let me know that nothing would be so dark that He wouldn't send the sun to light my way. Sweet little reassuring things to convince me that I WOULD make it through this and be victorious over this battle, because He had a plan for my life.

There was one day, that if it weren't for those "Little Hugs From God" I had been receiving along the way, I may have crumbled under the heartbreak. I walked into my mom's room and saw her at her desk reading something. I couldn't quite hear what she was saying. It was like she was studying something. When I spoke she was startled and tried to hide what she was doing. When I asked her about it she hesitated for a moment and then asked me if I would help her. I told her sure I would, and asked how I could help. She handed me this yellow piece of paper. On it she had written one letter of the alphabet on each line and a word beside it that started with that letter. She said she had been studying this every day and was trying to memorize it because she was having some problems remembering things sometimes. That day she told me with her eyes that she knew what was wrong with her. My throat began to tighten and I felt warm tears begin to fill my eyes. She asked me if I would help her study these words everyday. I told her I would study them with her as much as she wanted me to. She was absolutely thrilled. We both sat down on the bed and I would give her the letter "a" and she was supposed to tell me the word "apple." Of course she couldn't remember the words and I could see she was going to have a meltdown, so I would begin giving her clues, easy clues, to help her say the right word. We did that every day for about a week. I helped her just like she asked me to, until one day she no longer asked.

I would be lying if I said I never had dark times or times of questions and frustration. I did. I remember getting so frustrated at some of my mom's family because they absolutely refused to believe that my mom had Alzheimer's. Every time I talked to them they were convinced the doctor made a mistake because there was nothing wrong with her. This went on for almost three years. Didn't they think if I wasn't convinced the right diagnosis had been given, that I would have taken her to doctor after doctor until I knew the truth? It infuriated me. Why couldn't they see that they were only hurting me and my mother by choosing to stick their heads in the sand and not see the truth. It was as if they were calling the doctor, and me, a liar.

I got frustrated the day an insurance check to repair our van came up missing off of my desk. We searched the house from top to bottom. I asked mom fifty times if she had seen it or did anything with it because I would catch her shuffling papers on my desk occasionally. We looked inside and outside for hours. Finally, my husband started going through the trash and there it was. Mom had gotten it off my desk and crumpled it up and threw it in the trash.

For I can do everything through Christ,
who gives me strength
Philippians 4:13

stone 18

new day, same sorrow

The faithful love of the Lord never ends!
His mercies never cease. Great is his faithfulness;
his mercies begin afresh each morning.
Lamentations 3:22-23

Once again, I found myself riding on a train that got derailed. Even in the destructive aftermath of the crash, I found that God was still the one constant thing in my life that kept my JOY intact.

My husband's company laid off ten thousand employees and he was one of them. Right in the middle of a work day he was called in and told his services were no longer needed. After a year and a half of being unemployed God finally told us where He wanted us to go. We ended up moving closer to my brother because I knew I wanted him to get to be around mom as much as he could for the rest of her life. The day before we went to get the moving trucks I took mom back to the doctor because she had been limping for about a month and I wanted her to get checked out again before we left. We had done ultra sounds looking for blood clots and x-rays of her hip and knee but nothing was showing up. So that day we went and I told the doctor she was still limping. The nurse asked if they'd ever x-rayed her foot. I told her no, but let's do it. We were all shocked to find out that her heel was broken. We don't know when or how it happened. I felt horrible that she had suffered for a month because she couldn't communicate to me where she hurt. They put her in a temporary cast and told me to get her to a doctor when we arrived at our new home. They also told me I had to make sure she remained non-weight bearing on that foot for eight weeks. I almost laughed in the doctor's face. I couldn't imagine how in the world I was going to keep her in a wheelchair for eight weeks. I could not wrap my mind around the fact that I was going to have to keep her from standing on that foot for eight weeks. I almost laughed hysterically thinking of this happening the day before we were moving three and a half hours away.

We made the move and got her to a doctor. The hard part was keeping her in the wheelchair. Even with her leg extended on a leg rest she would try to stand up. Then we would have to get her to the bathroom and try to get her sat down quickly so she wouldn't try to take off walking. One day she got upset in the bathroom and stomped my bare toes with her cast. That was a very, very long eight weeks.

We also got a hospital bed for her when we moved. There were side rails but nothing over the head or foot of the bed. We found out the first night she could crawl over the foot of the bed and get out. So we ended up putting the head of the bed against the wall and my husband built a tall table that we placed over the foot of her bed. It was too tall for her to climb over it and she couldn't move it because the front two legs were on the inside of the footboard and the back two legs were on the outside of the footboard. It work out perfectly. We invented many things along the way to meet each new need we discovered.

Looking back, it is simply incredible how God was in control and took care of all our needs supernaturally. When we went to look at houses before we moved, my husband was still unemployed. The real estate agent was concerned about him not having a job and our ability to get a loan. I told her not to worry about it and for her to do her job and God would do the rest.

It was absurd to think we would be able to get a loan with no job and we were told that very thing by a bank. They said come back after he'd been employed for at least two years and then maybe they'd talk to us. Still, I wasn't concerned. I know it sounds unbelievable, but I was at perfect peace.

One day, a gentleman from one of the banks was in the real estate office. As he was leaving, he asked if there was anything else he could do for anyone. Our agent's boss was standing there and very sarcastically said, "Yeah, get someone a loan that hasn't had a job in a year and a half," she smugly chuckled. He stopped and turned around and said, "Give me their name, something came across my desk this very morning." My phone rang that day and I was absolutely dumbfounded to find out I knew the man on the other end of the phone from 25 years before. He knew my parents and my whole family. He told me that he would be able to get us a loan. No one will ever be able to tell me God doesn't exist or God doesn't have control over every single aspect of our lives.

As we settled into our new home, some things weren't new at all. One of those things was the change from the move caused another acceleration in my mom's disease. At this point, she had been diagnosed for three and a half years and could have actually had the disease at least five years before she was diagnosed. It certainly was progressing along. I remember the doctor telling me the better health a person is in when they get Alzheimer's, the longer they can live. My mother was walking five miles every day and was in great health when she was diagnosed. I couldn't help but wonder how much time I would have with my mom. I couldn't help but wonder if I would know how to care for her needs as they became greater.

Seek his will in all you do,
and he will show you which path to take.
Proverbs 3:6

I wanted my mother to remain as independent as safety would allow, for as long as possible. However, it didn't take me long to learn that something was going to have to be done to keep her safe and still allow her to have some freedom. We had stairs in the new house we bought and lived in a subdivision. The last thing I wanted was for her to fall down the stairs or get out and get lost. I couldn't even go to the bathroom if someone couldn't stay right with her. She was fast and could be gone in a minute. One day I was cooking and mom was pacing around the kitchen with me. I turned around and when I turned back she was just inches from putting her hand down in boiling water. Something had to be done. I asked my husband to go and get a cheap interior door. When he got home I asked him to cut it off about chest high. We took off her whole door and replaced it with this three quarter door and put a hook and eye on the outside of it. This way, I would know she would stay safe in her room if I needed to go downstairs or go to the bathroom and she still had freedom to walk all around her room and look out her window and listen to her TV or radio. I could see her at all times when she was in there. It was an answer to my prayer. She seemed happy with it too. She was still out with me the majority of the time, but it was nice to have this option if I needed to run get the mail or talk on the phone. This was another one of those inventions we came up with because we had a need. She also was able to have some freedom outside because we had a fenced in backyard. We would go out with her and let her walk and enjoy the sunshine. She got to listen to the birds, watch the squirrels, and even feel the grass between her toes. She couldn't be left alone, but she still had some freedom. It was so sad to watch her walk all around the fence shaking it like she was trying to get it to open. Everything this disease did to her was sad. Horribly sad.

When we first moved into our new home I decorated mom's room up and hung things on the walls. It didn't take long for me to realize I wasn't going to be able to do that. One by one, she took them off the wall and destroyed them. So eventually her walls were bare and I left them that way. She also found a tiny black spot on her wall and before I knew it she had dug through the dry wall with her finger.

Her strength was unbelievable at times. Before she got Alzheimer's she had problems with some arthritis in her hands. At times she couldn't even wring out a washcloth. Now, it was just the opposite. She had a death grip that even my husband couldn't break at times. She would get one of my thirstystone coasters and snap it in two like it was a cracker. So I bought some safe items I thought would help her keep her hands busy. One of those things was a Rubik's Cube. I just knew she would enjoy twisting and turning it. So I bought it, brought it home, handed it to her and I walked out to throw the trash away. When I got back I was stunned. There were only four little squares on the whole cube left. The rest of the pieces were all in her lap. All that was left was something that resembled a cross with a little colored square on the top, bottom and each side. She couldn't have had it more than three minutes. I couldn't figure out what she had done to get it apart like that. I couldn't have done it if I was trying.

Twice she took out her bottom denture and snapped it in two. Eventually I couldn't leave her dentures in except to eat because she would take them out and hide them or break them. I knew there was no way she could ever handle getting an impression made at the dentist if we had to get new ones made for her. Many times I would holler for everyone to come help me play "find the dentures." I'm not telling this to show any disrespect to my sweet mother, whatsoever. I would never do that. I did promise to tell the real truth, good or bad, happy or sad. This is one of those truths. People may not have even considered that these types of things would ever become an issue when caring for someone with Alzheimer's. I had to learn the hard way.

For the first 5 years after diagnosis we continued to take her to church with us every Sunday. Of course it became increasingly evident we wouldn't be able to do that forever. There were times she would get irritated because I would have to repeatedly stop her from reaching for the hair of the person in front of us, or their purse, bible, shirt, or back pocket. She would yell out in frustration and then when I would try to quiet her she would even get louder. One Sunday, after me pulling her hand back at least fifteen time from grabbing the people in front of us, she got so angry she screamed out, "Well s**t." You could have heard a pin drop. I wanted to crawl under the chair in front of me. Instead, I took her hand and led her out to the front and we waited for the service to end. She would have died from embarrassment if she would have known she said that.

She would answer the pastor, out loud, if he ever posed anything as a question. Sometimes she wouldn't give a very nice answer either. More than once I would take her by the hand and lead her out to the front and we would sit there and wait for the service to get over.

It was very difficult to get her up, bathed, fed, dressed, hair fixed, make-up done and in the van on Sunday mornings. Sometimes getting her into the van was like trying to get a bobcat through a doggie door made for a chihuahua. She would be clinging, with her death grip, on the sliding door of the van while we were pleading with her to let go and trying to get her lifted up into the van. However, the importance of us continuing to take her to church, far outweighed how difficult it was for us to get her there.

Another thing I discovered about Alzheimer's is that it takes your sweet loved one and eventually transforms them into a state where they are just like a helpless infant. In the end it was every bit the same for me as when I cared for my newborn baby girls.

Alzheimer's also brings out things in a person that would be totally opposite of the person's personality before they got sick. They can become physically violent, hateful in the way they speak to you, strong and destructive or use bad language they never would have before.

Death, was not when this disease took my mother away from me. I lost her one little piece at a time, every single minute, of every single day, from the day it first came to live in her brain.

I hated the disease that caused me to have to emotionally detach myself from my own mother, just so I could continue to care for her without losing my mind. It hurt my heart too much to look at her as my mother sometimes. So, many, many times I would have to look at her as a nice woman I was taking care of instead of my mother, just so I could get through that moment. Some may not understand this at all. Some may understand it only too well.

For I can do everything through Christ,

who gives me strength.

Philippians 4:13

stone 19

more sand in the bottom

You have decided the length of our lives.
You know how many months we will live,
and we are not given a minute longer.
Job 14:5

═∞═ ═∞═ ═∞═

God so blessed me by sustaining my mother's sweet, happy spirit throughout this whole nightmare. Not that there weren't bad times, there were. How thankful I was that she would smile at me, hold my hand and laugh out loud at times right up to the very end. I would sit at her feet and lay my head in her lap, crying at times, and she would pat my back as if she were comforting me. She wouldn't remember it a second after she did it, but I did. I'll remember it forever.

One Christmas I handed her a gift and she didn't know what it was or what to do with it. She would just hold it and smile at me. I would tear the paper with her hands but she didn't understand at all. She wasn't able to talk in a complete sentence or communicate her thoughts to me at all. I was so frustrated. It just broke my heart. I fell at her feet and put my head on her lap and just cried and cried. All of a sudden I felt her hand on my head and I looked up at her. She looked right into my eyes and said, "It's ok, I'm just broken." Then she looked off out the window like I wasn't even there. I simply fell apart. For her to say those exact words out of nowhere was one of those "Little Hugs From God" just for me.

She was so restless at times and it was completely out of her control. It was horrible to watch. She had to be doing something with her hands at all times. She would walk miles and miles in the house day and night. I felt like she needed "things" to busy herself with. So in her room I put a chest of drawers and filled every drawer with old clothes, towels, pillow cases, etc. That way she could open and close the drawers as many times as she wanted and take the clothes out and put the clothes back. She could fold and unfold as long as she wanted to. I also bought some toys that were colorful and safe to put in the drawers. I got stacker rings, stuffed animals, baby dolls, stackable plastic cups and plates, plastic laundry baskets, a beaded toy similar to an abacus, and so many more. I really don't have the words to express how I felt having to go to the toy department to buy birthday, Mother's Day, or Christmas presents for my mother. It broke my heart. It just wasn't supposed to be that way.

I learned as I went along on this journey. "On The Job Training" has a whole new meaning for me now. I remember the day that I looked over and it looked like mom had something in her mouth. She wouldn't open her mouth for me, so I stuck my finger in her mouth and pulled out a button from the blouse she had on. Lesson learned that day: she could no longer wear clothing with buttons. Zippers were no better because she wouldn't keep them zipped.

I found it interesting that I was able to guage where she was in her memories by the things she would say, as I watched her regress. At first, she would say all of our names as she would chatter to herself or if we walked into the room. Then one day she started acting like she was smoking a cigarette. My mom smoked for years but had quit smoking over twenty years ago. She would act like she was smoking and knocking the ashes off. One day my husband saw her doing that, left the room and came back with a clean, empty tuna can. He handed it to her and said, "If you're going to smoke you need an ash tray." I couldn't believe that he thought to do that. How precious he was to her as he helped me care for her every need, every day. He was my greatest help-mate and friend during this excruciating time of my life. Mom pretended she was smoking, and used that old tuna can as her ash tray, for a few weeks and then one day she stopped. That part of her memory had been stolen from her too. It was gone.

She would talk about her siblings that were still alive. Then, a month or so later, she would be talking about her siblings that had passed away. I was shocked one day when she spoke her little brother's name, Donny. He had died when he was just a little bitty boy and she was a very young girl. The most difficult part for me was when she started calling me "Mommy." Every time she would call out to me and call me "Mommy" my heart would sink a little deeper. I never corrected her and I always answered her every call. It may have been with tears running down my face, but I always answered her every call.

I could see her slipping further back in time. As if she was walking off into the horizon. I watched her get smaller and smaller until she faded away completely. I couldn't stop her and I couldn't run fast enough to catch up to her. I simply had to watch her go. I had to watch her leave me forever.

I would catch myself wondering how certain things were going to happen that hadn't happened yet. I began to think about how she was going to become incontinent. I had no idea how it was going to happen. Then one morning mom was standing in her room and I was putting away some of her clothes when all of a sudden I heard this noise. I looked around to see her going to the bathroom standing right there with no expression on her face at all. I got her changed and cleaned up her carpet. Later on that day it happened again and that early evening it happened again. When my husband got home I told him I didn't know what's going on. He asked me if I thought I needed to get some of "THOSE THINGS," and I told him I didn't know. He took me to the store and we both stood in front of the shelf and cried. I had no idea what to get. I certainly never thought I'd be standing in a store picking out Depends for my mother. I cried as I took each one down and read about them. My husband held me and cried with me in the store that night, then we bought a bag, went home and put one on my mom. From that day on she was incontinent. It had happened in one day. Suddenly, I realized there was more sand in the bottom of the hour glass of my mother's life, than there was in the top.

At that time I had to make a very difficult decision to stop taking her to church. I couldn't stand the thought of her sitting in church and having an accident. She would have rather died than to have known that happened. I knew that thieving disease would steal every memory she ever made, cause her to forget who she was, forget who I was and not be able to care for herself. However, as along as there was breath in my body I wasn't going to let that stinking, thieving disease rob her of dignity. Not going to church didn't end my relationship with God by any means. The church building is not what determined my relationship with God in the first place. Our relationship continued to grow every day right where I was. After all, He lived within me, how could He not be wherever I was. God knew what was happening. None of this caught Him by surprise.

I don't know how many times I was asked how we did it. How did we go on day after day, month after month and year after year. My answer was always the same. There were two things that carried us through this nightmare. The first thing, was the fact we didn't have to depend on our strength to do it. If that were the case I would have curled up in a fetal position and pulled the world in around me years ago. God is where our strength came from each and every day, each and every minute. He gave us the ability to do whatever we needed to do every second. He was the only thing we could count on to never change. He was the same yesterday, today, and forever.

The second thing was laughter. Now that may sound odd to some, but not to us. Laughter was always an important part of my childhood, life, family, and marriage. Laughter is how we got through the toughest of times. Now don't get me wrong. There's NOTHING, I repeat, NOTHING FUNNY ABOUT ALZHEIMER'S, but we felt a healing within ourselves each time we would allow laughter in our lives. So we made a pact as a family, to laugh together every day and laugh together we did. It may have been in the middle of tears, but we blended those tears with laughter.

A time to cry and a time to laugh.
A time to grieve and a time to dance.
Ecclesiastes 3:4

Another thing I discovered about Alzheimer's is not only does it alienate friends and family from the person with the disease, but it also alienates friends and family from the Caregivers. There were friends and family that I hadn't heard from since my dad's funeral. Even after they knew mom was sick, they didn't call. I understand how life goes on for everyone. I understand how everyone has their own things to deal with. I wasn't really angry with anyone, just lonely sometimes. There were many, many days just a simple phone call to let me know I wasn't alone and that someone was thinking about us would have really meant a lot. Just a phone call to allow me to feel "normal" for a few minutes. Someone to talk to that would let me feel like I had a life that went beyond Caregiving and Alzheimer's. Maybe we could have talked about things we'd done or places we'd been. Maybe just a little conversation about ANYTHING other than Alzheimer's would have made that day a little easier for me to walk through.

No one will really know what our lives were like unless they lived it for themselves. We didn't spend our days feeling sorry for ourselves or throwing ourselves pity parties, but we had no choice but to live in the reality of our situation. There were days I felt I made it through unscathed. But I'd be less than honest if I didn't tell you there were days I would scream into a pillow or think about getting in the car and driving far, far away from everything.

There were days that I was certain I could do it. There

were days I was certain I couldn't do it. There were days I was certain I didn't want to do it. But every day I was absolutely certain that I was Blessed beyond measure, for being given the privilege to do it. Many times the only way I made it through a day was to look back and see that I made it through yesterday. That gave me the confidence to know, with God holding my hand, and sometimes even carrying me, that I would make it through that day too. He saw to it that I always made it through.

I know that God did not give my mother Alzheimer's. Satan is the one that comes to steal, kill, and destroy, and destroy is what he intended to do to my entire family. He intended for his evil to destroy my mother, my marriage, my family, my physical health, my emotional health, and most importantly, my relationship with God. Instead, as a family, we were able to claim VICTORY over the enemy's repeated attempts of mass destruction. We did so with the power we were given over the enemy in Jesus's Name. We had found the key to winning the battle with the enemy and our family remained in tact. We would not be destroyed.

Look, I have given you authority over all the power of the enemy, and you can walk among snakes and scorpions and crush them. Nothing will injure you.

Luke 10:19

Many days I found myself shouting at the enemy to stay under my feet where he belonged. I told him he would NOT have control over my life, my circumstances, or my situation. He would NEVER ever rule or reign over my life. I told him to get behind me and that he must go in Jesus's Mighty Name. There is, indeed, life in the power of the tongue. It matters what we speak out loud. There is death, just like there is life, in the power of the tongue so we need to be very careful what we let come out of our mouths. We must speak God's Word over everything in our lives. If you find yourself in the most desperate time of your life and you can't utter a single verse from the Bible, just speak the name, JESUS. Just say JESUS. There is Power in His name. There is Strength in His name. There is Peace in His name. There is Joy in His name. There are answers in His name. There is Love in His name. There is Forgiveness in His name. His name is above ALL names.

For I can do everything through Christ,

who gives me strength.

Philippians 4:13

stone 20

second promise made

For we know that when this earthly tent we live in is taken down (that is, when we die and leave this earthly body), we will have a house in heaven, an eternal body made for us by God himself and not by human hands.
2 Corinthians 5:1

≡∞≡ ≡∞≡ ≡∞≡

Along with the final stage of the disease came some new challenges for us to embrace. I chose to look at it as just more "On The Job Training" for me.

I took my mother to the doctor every three months up until the last months of her life. There were times I wondered if my Caregiving was adequate. After all, I didn't have anything to compare it to. I was so relieved when the doctor told me at one visit that he was absolutely convinced that my mother would have died years before if it weren't for the love and quality of care she was receiving from us at home. As I heard those affirming words, I stood there and cried. What a

Blessing it was for me to hear that. I know that all the extra years her life was prolonged was for a great reason. I know it was because God was still doing a tremendous work in me, and my mom's work on earth was not yet done. Even the darkness of Alzheimer's couldn't stop her light from shining.

I took great pride in knowing that the entire time my mother was in my care, she never had a single issue with skin breakdown or one bed sore anywhere on her body. How sad it was, that it was those types of things that had to bring about great rejoicing for me.

Along with Alzheimer's came the common problem of frequent Urinary Tract Infections. Getting someone with Alzheimer's to urinate in a cup is just NOT going to happen. I knelt many times on the clinic's bathroom floor crying because I had been in there for 30 minutes or more trying to collect a urine sample for the lab to test. It was just impossible. Eventually, I asked the nurse if I could have one of the "hats" they use in hospitals to collect urine in so I could collect the sample at home on her portable toilet. Then all I had to do was take it to the lab. I became quite astute at knowing when my mom was getting a U.T.I. I was able to catch them right in the beginning stages before they made her terribly ill.

Meals and taking pills became a challenge as she got worse because chewing and swallowing became more difficult for her to do. I was determined that my mom would have nutritious, well-balanced meals every single day. We had to keep her immune system built up and her bowels working.

We cooked all kinds of vegetables for her and gave her lots of fruits. My daughters were a huge source of strength and help during it all. Chelsea had perfected the way to prepare and mash everything up so she had good nutritious meals. Now, getting her to open her mouth was a different story. Lacy found that if she put a bite of food on her spoon, dipped the tip of her bite in applesauce and rubbed it on her lips, she would open her mouth to lick the applesauce off of her lips and she could put the bite in her mouth with a little maneuver she invented that we called, the "Wiggle-Waggle." Mealtime was very tedious and time consuming but well worth the hard work. Any pills she had to take had to be crushed and put in applesauce. Every aspect of Cargiving was a true family affair.

It was unbelievably sad for me when she couldn't communicate with me any more. I learned to watch her body language so I would know if something was wrong. She would rub her temples or hold her head sometimes and I would know she had a headache and I would give her Tylenol. She would rub her neck, elbows, or hands and if the weather was cold or raining I would know her arthritis was bothering her and give her some ibuprofen. She couldn't tell me if she was thirsty, hungry, hot, cold, tired, or sick. We just kept her on a schedule and offered her drinks all the time.

It was awful to have to listen to her yelling or crying out all day long. Worse than that, was having to listen to it all night long. We would wheel her to her bed, do all of our bedtime things, get her all tucked in and I would pray over her. Then I would kneel beside her and lightly stroke her face to try to get her to relax enough to fall asleep. Sometimes she would fall asleep for an hour, then just about the time I was drifting off the yelling and crying out would begin. She would do that for hours, sometimes all night long I would get up and go in and try to get her settled back down and stroke her face, but it was as if someone wound her up with a key. Many, many nights I would lay in bed with my pillow over my ears, crying and praying to God to please give her peace through the night. Just for her to sleep. I would gladly listen to it the other sixteen to eighteen hours a day if she could just be able to rest peacefully for a few hours at night.

Along with the difficulty in swallowing came bouts of Aspiration Pneumonia. Seven bouts in her last year. No matter how careful we were, she would get strangled when she would take a drink at times and days later end up with Aspiration Pnuemonia. I would begin to hear her breathing change. It sounded like she was breathing liquid. Then all of a sudden she would begin to projectile vomit mucous everywhere and become extremely lethargic. The medications, breathing treatments, oxygen, drops to put under her tongue every few minutes, and suction would then begin for the next several days. A routine I had become quite familiar with, and one I wished I would have never had to learn.

Urinary Tract Infections and Aspiration Pneumonia

became fairly common in our home. However, we had one episode that had everyone confused, even the doctors. One day I could tell mom just wasn't feeling well. No real symptoms, just not herself. So I called the doctor and took her into see him. The doctor looked her over and suggested we take her to the hospital. He walked out to get her orders ready and while he was gone mom began to have seizures. We didn't know that's what they were at that time. I went out and got him. I told him she was doing something she'd never done before. He walked in and took one look at her and told us to get her to the hospital immediately. I asked him if she was dying and he told me no, we just needed to get her to the hospital as soon as possible. We rushed her to the hospital and my husband and I got her in bed. I raised her bed up and she continued to have one seizure after another. A couple of nurses finally came in and were standing at the foot of her bed asking me questions. Suddenly, Mom had a severe seizure and I watched the breath leave her body. The nurses were so busy talking to each other they hadn't noticed. I told them she stopped breathing and they frantically began to try to figure out what to do and who they should call. The whole thing caught me completely off guard. I had not even thought about what measures should or should not be taken in this type of event, because I honestly didn't think she was that close to dying. I don't know why, but I began to lower the head of her bed as the nurses were running around like chickens with their heads cut off. At that moment I heard a huge gasp and mom began breathing on her own, with no one doing anything to her. By that time the room was full and everyone was firing questions at me. She spent three days in the I.C.U. and we all thought she was going to die. She was in Atrial Fibrillation and basically comatose for two days. They ran every test imaginable and everything came back normal. No one could tell us what had happened or why. She was moved to a floor for three more days and then released. She was back to her old self again with no explanation. For the rest of her life I felt like I was walking on egg shells, waiting for the "next" thing to happen. I was always waiting for "the other shoe to drop."

God hears my cry. I love the Lord
because He hears my voice and prayer for mercy.
I will pray as long as I have breath.
Psalm 116:1-2

It was Monday, the week of Thanksgiving, when the "next," or maybe I should say, "last" thing happened.

Within an hour of feeding mom her breakfast she began to vomit. Yes, another round of Aspiration Pneumonia. I called and got the medicines and began the routine of all the treatments. She was very lethargic and slept in her recliner in the kitchen, with me keeping an eye on her and giving her drops every few minutes. Holidays really hadn't been the same for me since my dad went to Heaven, but I always went through the motions and did it for my family. I began talking to Mom about what I was going to fix for Thanksgiving dinner. I talked about our Thanksgivings from the past and how delicious her meal always was. I told her I was going to be baking the pumpkin pies in a day or two. I talked to her as I made cornbread for the dressing she always prepared. I always talked to her even though she couldn't talk back to me. I was never convinced that she couldn't understand some of the things going on around her, even though she was unable to respond to them.

I had no idea that this bout of Aspiration Pneumonia was going to be different than any of the other ones. I continued to care for her as I always had. Giving her baby spoons of Pedialyte, medications, breathing treatments, oxygen, and suctioning. Thanksgiving was the last thing I wanted to think about, much less prepare for. Any time she was sick like this I slept in a chair beside her until it passed. I didn't want her to lay flat on her back, vomit and aspirate.

She couldn't eat or drink. She wasn't going to the bathroom hardly at all. She was dehydrating and growing weaker and weaker. She could not stand and bear her own weight. I fought the thoughts that were trying to enter my mind. She had always bounced back no matter what she went through. I just knew she would bounce back this time too. Or maybe I just hoped she would bounce back.

Thanksgiving Day came and went. I fixed turkey and all the trimmings, but didn't really enjoy the meal at all. I would cook for a while and take care of mom for a while. I would look at her and couldn't help but think that this was going to be the last Thanksgiving I would have my mom with me. I don't think any of my family wanted to do the whole "Thanksgiving Thing," but we did it for each other.

When the week-end came, I watched as she seemed to slip a little further toward the point of no return. I remember a moment when I was sitting beside her and saw a look on her face. She had not been able to put a sentence together or respond verbally for a long time. She would moan or occasionally say yes or no, but nothing that was real communication. As I sat there I leaned over and gave her a kiss on the cheek and said, "Are you feeling bad mom?" I never expected an answer because she had been unable to do that for months. Just as I asked her that, she looked me right in the eyes and said, "I just want to die." You could have knocked me over with a feather. My husband was right there with me and I looked up at him and we both broke down. Those were the last words my mother ever spoke to me. I knew she was ready to go "Home." Now the question of the day was, would I be ready for her to go "Home?" I will always consider those words she spoke to me, out of the darkness that day, just another one of my "Little Hugs From God."

She had not been able to sleep in her bed that whole week. She and I had spent the nights together in recliners in the kitchen. She slept most of the time and could not eat or drink. On Sunday, my husband helped me wash her hair and

I gave her a bed bath and got her all freshened up. He held her as I changed the sheet on her chair and then we got her all settled back down. I began to notice a difference in her breathing that afternoon and her eyes looked sunken and dull. That night as everyone went to bed they all gave mom a hug and kiss. My husband said he'd stay up with me, but I told him to go to bed because he had to get up early for work the next morning. I told him if I needed him I would come and get him. I really didn't think this night would be any different than the previous nights. I pulled my chair right up against her chair and turned on the TV. I held her hand and talked to her even though she wasn't able to respond. I talked about the childhood she gave me, the way she showed me how to be a lady, and the way she taught me to be a mommy. I relived all sorts of memories from our lives together with her. I cried and talked, then I talked and cried. After a few hours, I noticed her breathing changed again. It became very rhythmical, almost mechanical. Her chest would heave as she breathed in and out of her mouth. It reminded me of seeing my dad on a ventilator. As this went on I knew Mom's time here on earth was coming to a close and she was getting ready to receive her great reward. She would very soon be Praising God with the Angels, reunited with her husband, friends and her family. She was going to be walking those magnificent Streets of Gold and marveling at all the Glory of Heaven. Everything that had been stolen from her mind and body would be totally restored to complete perfection. There would be no more loss for her to endure. She would no longer be "BROKEN." She would finally be "HOME." Just the thought of "HOME" gave me goose bumps. She was getting ready to attend the greatest Family Reunion our minds could ever conceive.

I remember thinking back to when I was spending my last fleeting moments with my father. There seemed to be more of a frenzy or hysteria taking place than I was experiencing now. Maybe it had something to do with me being by myself this time. Maybe because his death came quickly and was more of a shock. With my mom, I had been watching her die, one memory at a time, for so many years. I could have called for my husband to come be with me, but I didn't. I felt such a peace fall over me and my mom. I found myself getting lost in the sweet, intimate time I was allowed to share with her. Sweet, intimate, and so bittersweet.

I wasn't afraid of what was going to happen to my mom, but suddenly I began to feel overwhelmed. The last eleven years came rushing over me. The grief I had lived with for so long was hitting me right between the eyes. I had tried to push it away for so long. Now it was bubbling to the surface. It was a culmination of so many losses in my life, perpetual grief for years and years, the impending loss that lay in the recliner right in front of me, and the wonderment of the future that lay before me, hidden by a thick fog that covered the road I was journeying down. It all just came to a head. Nothing was lying dormant any longer. I sat there with great anticipation, waiting for it to erupt.

I pulled my mom close to me and held her in my arms as I stroked her hair and talked to her. All the while wiping my falling tears off of her face. Her breathing was becoming erratic. I was praying and crying but I wasn't out of control. It was a very quiet and peaceful time. Just like I felt when I was facing the last moment of my dad's life, I began to wonder what I would do at her very last moment. How would I react? How was I going to feel, at the very moment, I became an orphan?

As I set there holding my mom, talking to her about Heaven, I said, " Mom, I love you with all of my heart. I am going to miss you horribly, but I want you to know that no matter how much my heart aches, I "**PROMISE**" you I will Celebrate you to Heaven. I have no clue where that came from. I had never used that phrase before. Later, I would find out exactly why that came out of my mouth. God would reveal it all to me later.

Suddenly, she took in a breath and as she let it out her whole body just went limp in my arms. I set there waiting to see if she was going to take another breath. I waited holding my own breath so I could hear her breathe. There was no sound. Nothing but the ticking of a clock filled the silence. I laid my head on her chest. There was still no sound. Immediately, I felt a lightness in my Spirit that I hadn't felt in a very long time. I lifted my hands toward Heaven and said, "Thank You Jesus for taking her home." I couldn't believe it, I was almost giddy. I could just see her bounding through Heaven's Gates. I could just see her laughing, and shouting and running to meet all those who were there to welcome her "Home." Just then I looked over at the clock, and I said out loud, "3:55 a.m." In that very moment I had fulfilled the First Promise I had made to my dad. It may have taken me eleven years to do it, but I did it. I hadn't thought much about that Promise, in all those years, until that very moment. Then it came flooding back into my heart.

Quietly, I turned off all the machines, took off the nasal cannula that was on her for oxygen, cleared everything away that was around her, washed her sweet face one last time and went to tell my husband. He came in and sat with me as I called my brother and the funeral director.

The funeral director did not get there until after 10:00 a.m. that morning. I had six long hours to sit there with my mom's body. I had a lot of time to think and a lot of time to listen to God's voice. The longer I sat there, the more detached I became to my mom's body. I was still learning something from this ordeal even in that moment. Isnt' it amazing how God can use any situation to teach us something? Some people thought it was horrible when they found out it took that long for my mom's body to be picked up, but it wasn't for me. I was actually greatful for that time I had that morning. I learned so much. Class was still in session for me.

For then the dust will return to the earth,
and the spirit will return to God who gave it. Ecclesiastes
Ecclesiastes 12:7

I would touch her body every once in a while and look at her face. I watched as her body laid there and did absolutely nothing. It was serving no purpose at all. Suddenly, I couldn't see my mom in that body any more. She was no longer there. I couldn't bring myself to call that body Mom. I could feel I was detaching myself from that body. I completely realized that once our soul goes to Heaven we have no more use for our body. It has no meaning or purpose. It's just an empty shell. Just like a shell that a hermit crab inhabits until it needs it no longer and then leaves it behind. It's empty. At one time it served a great purpose, but once the living thing inside of it left, it was empty and useless to that hermit crab.

Funerals changed for me at that moment. A Funeral is supposed to "Celebrate" the life of the person, not to celebrate the lifeless, empty body laying in a casket. The last thing I did for my mom was to Promise her I would Celebrate her to Heaven and at that moment I knew I wasn't going to have a traditional funeral service. I had been attending her traditional "funeral" for the past nine and a half years. For me to truly Celebrate her to Heaven would have been tarnished by having people gather together, that we hadn't even seen since my dad's funeral eleven years before, just to stare at that empty body. I wanted everyone to remember her life. To remember her laughing, talking, and loving her family. To remember the wonderful meals she prepared for her family with such love. To remember the crazy things she would do that made us all call her "Lucy." To remember her performing on our stage as Aunt Polly making people laugh. To remember her standing on that same stage, performing a recitation she did every night for sixteen years called, "The Three Rusty Nails." To remember her for her Joy. I didn't want the Celebrating to be tainted by everyone filing by a box that contained nothing but an empty shell in it. When my father went to Heaven I respected all the decisions my mom made and went through the whole "funeral" thing. I know every time I think of my dad, the first picture that pops in my mind is of his body in a casket. Then I can go beyond that and see him in other memories. Somewhere along the way we got it all messed up. The Funeral Directors are the ones who really "profit" from funerals. If we believe what we read in God's Word, we'd see just how bad we've messed it all up.

For I can do everything through Christ,

who gives me strength.

Philippians 4:13

stone 21

embrace change

Don't be afraid, for I am with you.
Don't be discouraged, for I am your God.
I will strengthen you and help you.
I will hold you up with my victorious right hand.
Isaiah 41:10

∞ ∞ ∞

Now you may think that after my mom went to Heaven that everything should have been over for me and my family. That we should have just been able to pick up where we left off ten years before. If only it would have been that simple. If only that would have been true.

I'll never forget a time when someone opened their mouth and I actually saw ignorance just fall out at my feet. One day, while my mom was still with us, this person overheard me talking to someone else about Alzheimer's and what all was involved with being my mother's Caregiver. After my conversation was over, this person walked up to me and said, "You're going to be so relieved when your mom dies." I almost punched them in the nose. I couldn't believe what they had said to me. RELIEVED??????? How could they possibly think I would be RELIEVED to not have my mom with me any more. My mouth fell open in utter disgust at what they said. All I could do was shake my head and walk away.

When you live like we lived for almost ten years, it takes time to transition back into the world and living a life that is your own once again. A long time. People didn't understand that for years and years the four of us were not even able to leave the house together. There were no dinners out. There were no trips to the store, or going to the movies. There was never a time when I went to the store or anywhere and I didn't call to check on mom. Even if I was out of the house for a moment, she was never out of my mind. Everything was planned around Mom. Every decision was made with her needs being met first. We woke every morning, put our feet on the floor and just went into autopilot. We went to Mom's room, changed and cleaned her up, stripped her bed and started one of many loads of laundry that we would be doing that day. We brought her into the kitchen and got her settled in her recliner and I fixed her breakfast. It went on and on from there until about 9:00 p.m. every night. We didn't have to think about what we needed to do. We just moved like robots, each doing the thing that we did best, to see that all of Mom's needs were met with Love.

The first time the four of us got into our van together it

actually took my breath away and I just burst into tears. Something that simple, that had been gone from our lives for so long, brought such joy and sorrow to my heart all at the same time that I couldn't stop the tears. We had totally erased things like that from our minds through the years because we didn't want to feel any more pain or allow a bitter seed to be planted in our hearts.

Our year of "Firsts" started only four days after my mom went to Heaven. It was her birthday. Even through my tears, I had to smile at the thought of what she must be getting to experience. No birthday celebration on earth could even begin to compare with celebrating her first birthday in Heaven with her husband, family, and friends. Talk about the "Party of All Parties." I had to rejoice for her, even though I cried for me. I was determined to fulfill my Second Promise. I was going to Celebrate her to Heaven.

Before I knew it Christmas was upon us. It hadn't even been a month since she left here. Honestly, our hearts just weren't in it, but we marched on anyway. I opened a gift from my daughters that touched me beyond words and was straight from God. It was a necklace. On it was a gold butterfly and the words, "Embrace Change." When I read that it was as if it were being shouted from a loud speaker. EMBRACE CHANGE!!! Immediately the four of us began crying. We all grabbed each other and held on for a wonderful group hug and cry. Those two words couldn't have been any bigger if they would have been plastered on a giant billboard.

That was the true starting point of us beginning our "New Normal" without Mom. Yes, ANOTHER "New Normal." I was back on the hamster wheel again.

I wore that necklace every day. I said those words to myself a hundred times a week. Then on the morning of January 1, 2010 those words became rooted in our spirits. My daughters and I found ourselves in the kitchen talking and having a little sad time together. I told them we needed to pray. We all grabbed hands and each one of us took turns praying for direction for our future, guidance in walking through each moment, strength to take the steps we would need to take every day, and the courage to, indeed, Embrace Change. It was a very special time for me that I will never forget. As we prayed and cried together that morning I honestly believe we each began to "Embrace Change."

He will wipe away every tear from their eyes,
and death shall be no more,
neither shall there be mourning, nor crying, nor pain anymore,
for the former things have passed away.
Revelation 21:4

We all purposed ourselves to "Embrace Change." Has it been an easy thing for us to do? No, it hasn't. Are we finished Embracing Change? No, we aren't. Will we ever be finished Embracing Change? No, we won't. How could two simple words etched into a pendant on a necklace sound so simple but be oh-so-complicated.

Things that we had not been able to do or refused to even think about for almost ten years, now had to be placed back into our lives. Carefully, masterfully, placed back into our lives as if we were assembling the petals of a beautiful flower. They would have been simple things to most, but they were monstrous things to us.

<u>Things like:</u>

- Learning how to make decisions without first considering Mom and her well-being.

- All four of us being able to walk out of the house together.

- Not reaching for my phone every time I left the house to call and check on Mom.

- Not automatically saying NO when someone asked us to do something or go somewhere with them.

- Falling asleep without keeping an ear out for any little noise, thinking something may be wrong with Mom.
- Putting our needs first for the first time in a long time.

As we found ourselves struggling in our transitioning, we would ask each other why it was so difficult. Not only was it difficult, but it wasn't something that was joyful for any of us. Then one day Chelsea said, "Mom, what we're going through is kind of like the "Stockholm Syndrome." At first I thought there was no way that could be true. Then the more I thought about it the more I realized that she was right. It was like we had all been held captive for ten years and suddenly been given our freedom. You would think we would have been overjoyed, jumped back into life, and had a wonderful time doing it. When in reality we wanted to be back in that little captive "compound" we had learned to live in so well. We felt like a fish out of water. That was what we knew. That was what was comfortable.

We all felt lost in this new world. We knew how to live our Caregiving life, but we weren't too sure how to live this new, unfamiliar life we'd just been handed. Both of our daughters basically lost their twenties in our Caregiving years. So in many ways it was as if they had just graduated from high school, even though their ages reflected something different. Many times during those years I told them they could leave, go start their own lives and get on with living. Always, they would tell me no. They said they started this journey with me and were not leaving until they saw it through to the end. How could I argue with such pure, giving, unselfish love? How could I ever thank them? How could I ever tell them how much I loved them. How could I tell them how just much I knew their sacrifices meant to their Nanny and Papa. That's "Unconditional Love."

All of our Caregiving years did not come without a price that we all had to pay. However, it was a price that I would gladly pay over and over again, to be given the honor of taking care of my mom.

Within the first three years I had been living with such stress that it caused my adrenal glands to produce an abundance of cortisol in my body. I really wasn't aware I was living in stress. I always thought of someone that was stressed out as walking around wringing their hands worrying about everything, and that certainly wasn't me. After a test at the doctor's office, I was told my body was producing so much cortisol it was off the chart on her paper. Then after another five years, the same doctor told me my adrenal glands had been so overworked, for so long, that they basically weren't functioning at all any more. I was now in "Severe Adrenal Fatigue." So I had escaped the nightmare of Alzheimer's with my sanity in tact, my emotions in tact, my faith in tact, my mind in tact, my marriage in tact, my family in tact, but my body had suffered. It caused me to gain weight that has been nearly impossible to get off. The tiredness I feel, even after waking up after a great night's sleep, is immobilizing at best sometimes. Then to hear there's not a quick fix for it and it could take years to get back to normal was not what I needed to hear. I had already put in so many years dealing with health issues. How many more would I have to face now?

The stress had affected us all, but we were unaware of it because we weren't taking it out on each other. We had gradually learned to cope with it because it had become part of our every day lives. It just goes to show you what a body and mind can get accustomed to.

For I can do everything through Christ,

who gives me strength.

Philippians 4:13

stone 22

beauty for the ashes

In his kindness God called you to share in his eternal glory by means of Christ Jesus. So after you have suffered a little while, he will restore, support and strengthen you, and he will place you on a firm foundation.
1 Peter 5:10

You may think that after losing my dad, losing my dream of our family business of sixteen years, losing thirteen years of my life, and losing my mom, that I would be throwing myself daily "Pity Parties." You may think I would be bitter or angry with what I'd been give to deal with. You may even think that any given day you would find me curled up in a dark room whimpering, whining and complaining about how my life was in ruins and how my purpose had been taken away from me. I can see where you may think those things.

I may even have thought those things if I was reading this book about someone else. I can even see how someone could feel that way that went through what I did. For me to try to explain why I didn't and don't feel those things is not an easy thing for me to do. I can only tell you that I didn't feel those things and I don't feel those things. I can't take credit for it. I can't even give all the credit to my tremendously, loving, unselfish daughters and husband. For something like this there is only one word that can even begin to explain it and one person that I can give the credit to, and that is GOD!

The past thirteen years have been riddled with sorrow, confusion, tears, frustration, helplessness, grief, and questions. Many, many questions. But through it all God wrapped me up in the sweetest blanket of Peace. Not the kind of Peace you deserve. Not the kind of Peace you can understand. Not the kind of Peace that can come from anyone, but God. It was a Peace in the middle of the most hideous, destructive storm that just let you know everything was going to be ok. I never doubted that God had a plan. I never doubted that it would all work out for His Glory. I didn't have to have all the answers, I only needed to draw close to Him. So that's what I did, and still do. I cling to Him daily.

Well, time continued steadily marching on, like a slinky down a staircase. The habits we'd developed over the past ten years were not going to go away very quickly. Caregiving habits, like we had established, don't just disappear. It was like we were having to be deprogrammed.

Slowly and cautiously we moved through the days, weeks and months. We had to learn to push away those sporadic pangs of guilt that would try to pop up sometimes, when we would be attempting to find joy in our new-found freedom.

Always be full of joy in the Lord. I say it again rejoice!
Let everyone see that you are considerate in all you do.
Remember, the Lord is coming soon.
Don't worry about anything; instead, pray about everything.
Tell God what you need, and thank him for all he has done.
Then you will experience God's peace,
which exceeds anything we can understand.
His peace will guard your hearts and minds
as you live in Christ Jesus.
Philippians 4:4-7

When we first moved my mom in with us I still was NOT playing, singing or listening to ANY music at all, and I hadn't for three years. It would be another year before that would change.

Then one day, God being who He is, knew I needed to share the gifts He had given me. So He caused the Joy of music to come alive again in my heart. I knew it had always been there. It never truly went away. It wasn't dead, it was just laying "dormant" like a volcano.

I find it so like God to have the very year my mother

was actually diagnosed with Alzheimer's and handed a death sentence, to be the same year music "erupted" in my heart again.

Music came alive for me again after we had been going to a small church for a while. God worked through some dear friends to help bring my gift back to life. My husband and I even ended up playing and singing on the Praise Team. However, this time, music felt different to me. It had changed, and it was for the good.

Two years later we moved back to Missouri. I knew my mother's life would be coming to a close and I wanted to be close to my brother so he could be with her throughout the rest of her life. I needed him with me now more than ever.

The disease wasn't the only thing that was progressing. So was my relationship with God. Every time the enemy tried to drag me down with the reality of that hideous disease, my strength and faith grew stronger. My thoughts were set on Him. I wanted to sing about Him. I wanted to talk about Him. I wanted to live Him.

One day, I was at home playing the piano and I found myself thinking about how Jesus came to earth. Since I am a mother, I began thinking about how I would have handled it if I would have been Mary. I began trying to put myself in her place. I started seeing things through Mary's eyes. How she must have felt and what she must have thought. The Joy and pain that was within her at the very same time. What an awesome responsibility she had placed on her. To be known as the mother of Jesus must have been more than she could have comprehended at that time.

Suddenly, I was playing music that I didn't know and had never played before. An overpowering rush of emotion came over me and I began to cry. It was as though there was a movie playing in my head. I grabbed a pen and began to write down the music and words that were coming to me as quickly as I could. I knew at that very moment, I was being given a gift by God. That was the day "Mary's Little Lamb" was breathed into existence by God.

Mary's Little Lamb
© 2005 Tonya Ferguson

On the day that He was born and she became a mother
Her heart was filled with love that day she knew was like no other
She had no way of knowing when she laid Him on the hay
Her perfect little baby boy would have a price to pay

Mary had a little lamb His fleece was white as snow
He was born to be the chosen one and Mary watched Him grow
And on the day he died, beneath her tears and grief she felt pride
Knowing her little lamb was Jesus Christ

How she felt at Calvary we can only wonder
Did she scream or did she plead as the crowd roared like thunder
She had no way of knowing when they came for Him that day
The price of sin for all men He was about to pay

Mary had a little lamb His fleece was white as snow
He was born to be the chosen one and Mary watched Him grow
And on the day he died, beneath her tears and grief she felt pride
Knowing her little lamb was Jesus Christ

That was the very beginning of my songwriting. Several songs have followed and many are yet to come. I've noticed that God gives me a song when He has a message for me to hear. That song helps me overcome what I'm going through at that time in my life. Every time I go through a struggle, a song will come. It will be bathed in the very words that will heal me, encourage me, and help me continue on my journey in Peace.

Sometimes I feel like I am a "Songcatcher" rather than a "Songwriter." I merely catch them as God drops them down to me from Heaven. My songs are so intimate to me, I sometimes feel very vulnerable sharing them with others because I HAVE LIVED THE SONGS I SING.

I noticed my songs didn't start coming until I was a Caregiver. Coincidence? NO WAY. It was like God was waiting until He had my full and complete attention before He started giving me songs. He wanted to make sure I was in a position to REALLY listen. He wanted me to HEAR what He had to say. I think He waited for me to become His captive audience. Captive, so I would sit still and get quiet. Quiet, so I could hear His sweet voice.

Be still, and know that I am God!
I will be honored by every nation.
I will be honored throughout the world.
Psalm 46:10

Because my songs seem to journal my life as I live it, I can look back and tell by the dates I wrote the songs, where I was in my journey. I became a "Songcatcher" the last four years my mother was here on earth with me. At that time in my life, my path was so overgrown with life's underbrush, there were days I struggled to barely take one step. My "relationship" with God grew so much in those years.

Sheepishly, I'll admit, I am a bit of a "Control-Freak." The greatest lesson I learned during all those years was there are things I CAN'T fix, CAN'T change, CAN'T make go away, CAN'T take charge of, CAN'T ignore, and CAN'T give away for someone to do for me. Ultimately, I learned I didn't have to deal with it all alone. This was NOT my battle to fight by myself. I finally learned to let go and lean. I let go and leaned on Jesus.

I am so thankful that as the list of my songs continues to grow, so do I. I am God's handiwork in progress. I am His clay that He is constantly molding and shaping.

Here is the list of the songs I've "caught" so far:

<u>In 2005</u>

Mary's Little Lamb

Unconditional Love

The Only One That Limits God Is You

No Greater Gift

In 2007

I Remember You

I Wasn't There

God's Love Won't End

He's In Everything

Lord, I Love You

Let's Take Jesus Off The Cross

It's Where You're Going That Matters

Praise Him Just Because

Out Of The Church

In 2008

One Day Soon

Gifts You Freely Gave

We're All Related By The Blood

He Never Stopped Loving

I Can't Make It On My Own

God Will

He's All We'll Ever Need

Always Take The Cross

Blessings In The Valley

God Can't Remember

The Silence Speaks

In His Presence

Seed Size Faith

I Don't Want To Have Regrets

God Makes Special Windows

Angels Are With You

Today I'll Marry My Best Friend

He'll Remove The Sting

Hanah's Prayers

The Curtain Of Heaven

Lord, Ready Me

Healing

My Precious Lord

God Will Take Us Through

One Prayer At A Time

In 2009

That Day

I Don't Know How

Take Me Back

What You Lost You Now Have Found

God's Garden

Grace Rain

Rise Up

If We Were Like Him

You're My Reason Now

Celebrate Them To Heaven

<u>In 2010</u>

I Thirst For You

Do You Know

One Nation Under God

In God We Trust

Love, God

God's Remnant

My El-Shaddai

Through You

No Storm

Beauty For The Ashes

Psalm 103

Come Broken

I'm Gonna Sing For My King

Free-Fall Of Love

My Footprint In Time

In 2011

His Touch

My Footprint In time

I'm Gonna Sing For My King

Freefall Of Love

Come Broken

Psalm 103

Beauty For The Ashes

To Remember Love

In August of 2009, I released a CD featuring ten of the songs I had written. I dedicated that CD to my mom. I believe with all my heart, that if I hadn't become her full-time Caregiver, I never would have written a single song. I really know that in my heart.

God has given me so much Beauty For The Ashes of my grief-filled life. That is another one of His sweet promises He gives us. I think one of the things I will always treasure most, is how God used those two promises to lead me to the "NOTES" in the ashes. All of those precious scribbled down "NOTES," that became lyrics, and the sweet sounding musical "NOTES," that became songs. All of those "NOTES" in the ashes have become the songs I've lived. In the charred ruins of my life, after excessive loss and grief, came beauty. God freely exchanged the ashes for beauty.

One of the songs I wrote tells what Caregiving and Alzheimer's was really like to live with every day. The first half of each sentence, in the verses, describes the different types of destruction that took place in my mother because of Alzheimer's Disease. The second half of each sentence describes the different ways I chose to be a Blessing as a Caregiver to my mother. In my heart, this song will always be my Caregiving Anthem to her. I wrote this song to honor my mom. I sing this song to remember my mom. I share this song with all Caregivers because I've lived this song and I want to help lift you up out of the darkness of your sorrow, and let you know you are not alone in this horrible battle.

I want you to know when the weight of sleepless nights, when living the same Groundhog Day year after year, when the loneliness sets in, when the frustration builds as you watch your loved one suffer and deteriorate, when the tears fall like rain, when you can't see tomorrow's joy for today's sorrow, when you want to give up, when you feel inadequate to be a Caregiver, when no one asks how you're doing, when you're screaming into a pillow, when all you feel is sadness, when you're overwhelmed by just waking up in the mornings, when you can't make sense out of your situation, just know that I walked those same footsteps you are walking, and together, with God's Grace, we will Conquer anything satan tries to throw our way. We are Caregivers hear us ROAR!

I Remember You
©Tonya Ferguson

When you don't know our name anymore,
we'll whisper it in your ear.
When you don't know your name anymore,
we'll say it when you're near.
When you don't know where you are anymore,
we will hold your hand.
When you're too weak to get up anymore,
we will help you stand.

Watching you die one memory at a time,
is as cruel, as cruel as cruel can be.
But one day soon your memories will be back,
They'll come flooding back, for all eternity.

When you don't know how to eat anymore,
we'll feed you every bite.
When you don't know how to sleep anymore,
we'll tuck you in at night.
When you don't know how to walk anymore,
we'll stay beside your bed.
When you don't know how to talk anymore,
we'll tell you what you've said.

Watching you die one memory at a time,
is as cruel, as cruel as cruel can be.
But one day soon your memories will be back,
They'll come flooding back, for all eternity.

When your eyes close that final time
and you're with our Lord and Savior.
Of all the things you'll say to Him,
you'll never have to say I can't remember.

When you are gone your memories will live on.
Your sweet and loving ways we'll cherish all our days.
When the time comes for us to come home too.
The thing we'll want to hear you whisper in our ear is......
I Remember You.

The moment I spoke that last Promise to my mom, I knew it would become a song. Twenty eight days after she went to Heaven, this song was born.

<u>*Celebrate Them To Heaven*</u>
© 2009 Tonya Ferguson

We will see loved ones go. Tears will fall sorrows show.
We may want to have an answer. We may ask our Father why.
If we scream out in our anger,
God will hold us while we cry.

When we must say goodbye. Their body goes but they don't die.
When they pass from here to Heaven,
And the gates swing open wide.
Eternal life that day is given,
There with Jesus they'll abide.

Let's Celebrate in our knowing. Celebrate who they will see.
Celebrate where they're going. Celebrate on bended knee.

If they saw how we mourned. And the grief that we wore.
They would say our life's not over. We must work until He comes.
Though our hearts will ache without them,
Their dusk on earth was Heaven's dawn.

So Celebrate them Heaven. Celebrate their going Home.
Celebrate them to Heaven. Celebrate till we go Home.

I found it amazing, that sometimes God would lay a song on my heart that wasn't about a personal struggle or situation of mine, but because of other people's struggles or situations. It may be the loss of a loved one, childhood cancer, Alzheimer's, the breakup of a family, a wedding, the devastation drugs and alcohol play on a family, or any other "real-life" thing. That's when I began to see that the songs I was being given by God, weren't just for me. Others could hear His voice in the songs too.

I was finally able to see that me going through everything I experienced was for a greater reason than I could have ever imagined. Other people are enduring horrible things in their lives too, but maybe they don't have a strong relationship with Christ or a strong family unit to get them through it. I began to realize that maybe the words God blessed me with during my dark, difficult times, could also encourage others while they were going through their own struggles. God showed me that the messages in my songs have no boundaries. They can reach out and speak to anyone that's ever experienced any "real life" struggle. That covers everyone on the face of this earth. Sadly, we're all members of that club.

I now stand on the other side of the longest and greatest thirteen-year-storm I've ever battled. I rejoice in knowing my purpose, now, is to plant a "Seed Of Need" in as many hearts as I can. My prayer is that seed grows and causes others to seek God's face and build their own relationship with Him.

As I travel and share my story in song and testimony, I am so proud to say it is a story of VICTORY and ENCOURAGEMENT. It is my prayer that this book will be an umbrella for you to hold on your stormiest days. You see, I know what it's like to find yourself in a deep, dark hole with the dirt crumbling in around you. But I also know Who's hands are holding the shovel that will dig me out every single time. Those hands only belong to my God, and His hands are there for you too.

I want to shout it from the mountain tops that there is never a time when it is ok to give up or quit. Nothing is impossible with God. The rewards for us fighting battles in our lives are being stored up for us in Heaven. We only live a mere moment on this earth, but we will spend Eternity with Jesus. I would much rather get my rewards later and have them last for an Eternity, than to get them now, here on earth, and have them only last for a moment. With God standing beside you, every battle is worth the fight. Just know, The Greater the Battle...The Greater the Reward.

Throughout my thirteen-year-storm, there were three things I learned that continuously held my head above water and never let me drown. Praise God, I have the peace of knowing those three things will be there for me forever, no matter what I may face in my future. God is the same TODAY, YESTERDAY and FOREVER! With Him ALL things are possible. He truly is my All in All and my Prince of Peace.

These are the things that I want others to grab ahold of and take away with them, from all of this:

1. "What God did for me in my life, He will do for you." God does not show favoritism. He is no respector of person. Romans 2:11

2. "Shadows can't exist without the light." What satan means for evil, God will turn it around for something good. Genesis 50:20

3. "Your battles may leave you standing in the middle of charred ruins, but never fear." God will give you Beauty for the Ashes. Isaiah 61:3

A dear, sweet friend had come to our home seeking a Safe Haven not too long before my mom went to Heaven. She observed us living our Caregiving life first-hand. We thought nothing of it at the time. Like I said, after all those years, we had gotten to the point that we were on auto-pilot from the time we woke up until we went to sleep at night.

She was watching the four of us prepare mom's food, put thickener in her drink, get her ready to eat and take turns feeding her. We weren't really talking about what we were doing, we were just doing it, just like we always did. I noticed she was getting emotional, and she began to cry. She said, "It's like I'm watching a beautiful dance. I love the way you all take turns caring for her. It's such a selfless love and you all need to say no words to each other, it's like you just know how to do your part." I couldn't believe anyone could see something so precious in our every day routine. We all began to cry and hug. She may never know just what that did for my family that day. That was a perfect example, of just one of the times, that God Gave Me Beauty For The Ashes.

I may have been the one that wrote this book, but I didn't live my story alone. My husband and daughters lived this every day right along with me. They had their own struggles, dark times, moments of chaos, and sadness to deal with too. No one came out of this nightmare the same way they went into it. All four of us carry scars from our battle. We may carry the scars, but we also carry the Victory of knowing we WON the battle we all so desperately fought.

I will never be able to replace the nine and a half years my daughters gave up. I will never be able to return to them what they lost. I know they did it with the right heart and for the right reasons, but at what cost? I could never "Pay It Forward" enough to begin to match what they did for me and my mom. If I were to lose them in the fall-out, it would be worse than everything I've lost in my entire life. I don't know how I could ever love or cherish them more.

To say I am married to the man that God created just for me would be an understatement. What he went through to bring his mother-in-law into his home and care for her for nine and a half years was more than most people would have done for their own parents. Never a grumble, never a complaint, never a regret passed from his lips. Only words of LOVE and ENCOURAGEMENT. I don't know how I could ever love or cherish him more.

I struggle miserably, trying to find something I can say or something I can do, to tell them or show them how much their sacrifices meant to me. There are no words to tell them. There are no actions to show them. The words "Thank You" are completely inadequate. All I can do is stand on God's promise that He will give my whole family a double portion of prosperity and everlasting joy to compensate us for our brokenheartedness, mourning, and suffering. He will give us "Double for our Trouble."

I have to believe that God, in all His mighty wisdom, knew the journey my family had walked was not to harm us, but help us. The enemy's plan was to see my husband and daughters destroyed. Thankfully, God is the Author of our lives and His Will is what defines us, not the enemy's. I can only pray, one day, all four of us will see the Plan that God has for each of our lives come to fruition.

I wanted others to understand that this experience affected the rest of my family too. They walked right along beside me. So I asked my husband and daughters if they would answer some questions for me.

Here are their answers:

Would you be the person you are NOW if you hadn't been a Caregiver for nine and a half years?

KEVON: "No. I had to take what I believe and put action to that belief. I had to die to self, suck it up, and keep my family encouraged and healthy, by believing in the dark what I learned in the light."

LACY: "No. It gave me a different outlook on life. It showed me that in a blink of an eye your whole world can be forever rocked. It taught me to value life more because you don't know what the future is going to bring or what's ahead that could change your life as you know it."

CHELSEA: "No. That would mean my journey would have taken a wrong turn."

Did being a Caregiver make you a better person? How?

KEVON: "Yes. I learned what was important and what was not. I purged out junk in my life and I welcomed new and witty inventions like the half-door or the way the food was prepared and served. I learned what problems really were and petty stuff didn't phase me. I had to choose everyday to reflect what Jesus would do."

LACY: "I don't think it made me a better person, but I do think it made me a different person. I don't know who I would have been without this experience, but I do know I wouldn't be the person I am today. I wouldn't be as caring. I wouldn't be as patient. I wouldn't be as strong and I wouldn't be as selfless."

CHELSEA: "It has strengthened and fine tuned the qualties I already had. It sharpened my already sharp coping skills. It taught me patience, perseverance, and the meaning of sacrifice. I know nothing is impossible. It has made me intolerant to selfishness, hatred, and any immature self-induced adult drama. I have compassion for the hurting and hopeless. My empathy knows no bounds. It has made people appear naked to me, because everyone has a story, but it's how the story ends that matters most. It gave me a backstage pass to what the human spirit is actually capable of."

What did you learn from your Caregiving experience?

KEVON: "I learned to give on purpose and chose to do what was right when no one was watching or telling me "good job." I learned my part that I could do and I just did it without complaining. I learned to laugh even when it wasn't funny to others. I learned what it means to Love Unconditionally. I lived Groundhog Day, every day. If I missed it one day I got another do-over the next day. I learned my daughters are ten times better than I could be."

LACY: "I learned that I am stronger than what I even knew, and to never doubt my abilities or what I'm capable of. I learned that through some of the most chaotic and scariest moments, is when I grew the most. I learned how to remain calm even when my world is spinning around me. I also learned what true inner strength is."

CHELSEA: "That, in a world of instant gratification, almost everyone has silenced their own ability to survive and overcome difficult journeys of any substantial length, but that anyone can endure anything if they're driven by faith, determination, and unconditional love."

What was the worst part?

KEVON: "When she couldn't remember her daughter or granddaughters, it was mind-numbing and so very sad. Especially, when I was expecting her to snap out of this disease and remember again. Or when Tonya had to put a pillow over her ears to cry herself to sleep from the hollering and non-stop yammering, (chattering), all night long. The very worst thing was I couldn't fix what was happening."

LACY: "Never knowing what was going to happen next. Not having any control. Watching her deteriorate in front of my eyes. Not being prepared to feel misplaced, lost, and disoriented after she passed away."

CHELSEA: "Seeing what it did to my mom THEN."

What was the best part?

KEVON: "In the beginning I looked for ways to make sense out of this disease. So when I took my mother-in-law outside to sit I would try to talk to her, and I discovered she couldn't remember what I had just asked her. That's when I asked God what good could I get from this. He told me to ask her what she knows about me, (Jesus). So I asked, and she said tell me. So I told her about Jesus many, many, many times. I used cheat sheets to share the Gospel with her, and the best part was I wasn't intimidated to talk to her. She helped me to know how to get people saved."

LACY: "Knowing that she was safe in our house and was being taken care of by people who loved her."

CHELSEA: "Seeing what it did to my mom NOW"

If asked, would you do it again?

KEVON: "To do it again for my mother-in-law, YES, gladly."

LACY: "Knowing all I know now, seeing all I learned from it, and knowing she was able to live out the rest of her years surrounded by love, yes, I would do it again."

CHELSEA: "I was never asked the first time, it was just a given. There was no answer to give. So, it's a given that I would do it all over again.

Describe Caregiving in one or two words?

KEVON: "Compassion."

LACY: "Unpredictable."

CHELSEA: "Unconditional Love."

That, is my family. The family that has learned how to love each other, forgive each other, laugh with each other, and help each other. The family that wants the very best for each other. The family that's happy if one of us is happy, and sad if one of us is sad. The family that my mom and dad created. The family that Love cemented together forever. The family that God holds dear to His heart. The family that shows me everyday that I am SO INCREDIBLY BLESSED!!!

I know God has changed countless lives by giving me the words to sing, that have spoken to many hearts. I know lives that were actually saved because of the path I've walked, and I give all the Praise and Glory to my Heavenly Father. To be the empty vessel for God to fill up and use, is a great Honor and Blessing.

If the pain I endured on my journey can prevent someone else from hurting, then it was worth it all. If the road I walked can show others where to step and not step, then it was worth it all. If my broken heart is what brought about the wonderful Blessings God has poured over me, so I could Bless others, then it was absolutely worth it all.

None of what I went through could even begin to compare with the anguish, torture, pain, torment, humiliation, and grief my Savior, Jesus Christ went through, so that I wouldn't have to. Not even when I held my mother and father as their last breaths were breathed. Just the thought of sending one of my children to have to live that horrible day, for people that have never even been born, leaves me speechless. I simply can't find the words.

His bright, red blood that covered the streets, land, and cross that day, is what blanketed me with pure white salvation and completely covered my sins forever. What an absolute unimaginable, undeserved, unthinkable, unmerited, and unearned Gift of GRACE God has given us. Do you want to know what the real kicker is? It's absolutely FREE. It doesn't cost us a single penny. I think we'd all agree, that if we had to watch one of our children die that horrific death, we certainly would expect someone to pay for it. We would want everyone that was going to benefit from it to have to pay for it, and pay dearly. I sure am glad we're not God, aren't you?

If you're reading this and don't know the kind of Peace, Love, Grace, Mercy, and Forgiveness I'm talking about, then please don't close this book until you make sure you do.

If you are stumbling, aimlessly, through life, with misery as your only traveling companion, then let me introduce you to the man called Jesus. He will walk every step with you for all eternity. No matter what you've done or what's been done to you in your past, it DOES NOT MATTER. All those things will be wiped from your life forever, as if they never happened. Your new, born-again, life will begin in this very moment. You will become a citizen of the greatest Kingdom ever created, the Kingdom of God. You will never be alone and you will spend eternity with Jesus, the one who came and died for you. What an awesome gift God wants to give you.

For God loved the world so much that he gave his one and only Son, so that everyone who believes in him will not perish but have eternal life.
John 3:16

Choosing to receive Jesus Christ, as your Lord and Savior, is the best and most important decision you will ever make in your entire life. God's Grace has already provided everything necessary for Salvation. Your part is simply to Believe and Receive.

The Bible, (God's Word), says...

If you confess with your mouth that Jesus is Lord and believe in your heart that God raised him from the dead, you will be saved. For it is by believing in your heart that you are made right with God, and it is by confessing with your mouth that you are saved. For Everyone who calls on the name of the Lord will be saved.
Romans 10:9, 10, 13

If you yearn for a type of Peace to live inside of you that defies definition. If you want Jesus to rule and reign over your life. If you want the Holy Spirit to come and live in you and guide you on your daily walk with Jesus, then all you have to do is ask. It's that simple. Just pray this prayer out loud.

Dear Lord Jesus,

I believe in my heart that You are the Son of God. That You died on a cross, and shed Your blood to forgive and cover my sins. I believe three days later You rose from the grave and conquered death.

Lord, I know I was born a sinner. Now I thank You for forgiving my sins and changing my heart to be like Yours, one that's filled with love, compassion, and forgiveness. I want to have a living Relationship with You. I believe You are alive and now live in me. I believe I am now saved from death and re-born a new creature. I thank You for sending people into my life that can help me on my new path. I receive You now as my Lord and Savior. Thank You for Your Love.

In Jesus' Name I pray, Amen.

If you PRAYED that and BELIEVED that, then you are a "Brand New You." You are a Kingdom Citizen, and promised eternity with Jesus. Seek out people that are born-again and surround yourself with them. Find a church to go to that teaches God's Word. Read your Bible. Pray ALL THE TIME. Prayer is merely talking to God. Just talk to Him.

This means that anyone who belongs to Christ has become a new person. The old life is gone; a new life has begun!
2 Corinthians 5:17

This is going to be the last chapter in my book. I said in the beginning I didn't know how it would end, because I wasn't there yet. Since I've been living this story as I was writing it down, I said the end may only be found when I come to a peaceful place in my heart and know that it is well with my soul. I was right. That's exactly what has happened. I HAVE come to a peaceful place in my heart, and I KNOW that it is well with my soul.

Just because my life didn't turn out the way I thought it would, doesn't mean it didn't turn out the way it was supposed to. When I made the choice to begin living in a meaningful relationship with Jesus Christ, my life was no longer my own. The Holy Spirit living inside me was my guide. I ended up just where God planned for me to end up, not where Tonya wanted to end up. I never would have chosen to go through what I've been through for myself. No one would have done that. I would have told you there's no way I could survive it. That wouldn't have been a lie, because Tonya, would not have been able to survive it. God and I, doing it together, is the only way I got through it without it destroying me. I now have opportunities I would have never had. I look at life so differently now. I'm more patient and empathetic. People have been put in my life that I never could have ministered to if I wouldn't have lived the life I've lived. I know I never would have become a Songwriter, or "Songcatcher," because I've lived every song I've written. My songs couldn't have been born without me living them first. I would not have become the Woman of God that I am today if it weren't for all my yesterdays. So what satan meant for evil, my God turned it into something Great, and oh so Blessed. God, indeed, has given me BEAUTY FOR THE ASHES.

I pray that in living my story I will bring others into the Kingdom of God. I pray my story will be an encouragement to anyone who reads it, and to know that what God did for me He'll do for you.

What began as a simple story about Unconditional Love, Promises Made, Promises Kept, Loss, Caregiving, Sorrow, Grief, Building a Relationship with God, and ultimately receiving the most wonderful Gift of finding my "Notes" in the Ashes, has ended in marvelous revelations being laid out before me.

I have learned the importance of keeping promises that I make. God has shown me that He is the greatest Promise Keeper of all, because my life is built on the Promises that He keeps with me daily. He has Promised me my life will never end and I can count on to Him to keep every Promise He has ever made.

I have learned how to give Unconditional Love to

someone that never asked for it. The greatest example I will ever have of Unconditional Love was freely given for my benefit, to hang on a Cross without me ever asking.

I have learned there is nothing more important than my RELATIONSHIP with my Father in Heaven and with His strength I CAN do ANYTHING. I've proven there is no limit to the strength I will have through Christ, by living this book. No matter what I've been through, no matter what I'll go through, at the heart of it all I AM BLESSED!

So, to anyone who's lost something or someone, to anyone that is swallowed up in grief, to anyone searching for the light in the darkness, to anyone that's sacrificed it all for the sake of someone else's well being, to anyone that's trying to keep a promise they made, to anyone that's lived days that feel like they're fifty hours long, to anyone that's lost time they'll never get back, to anyone that has a child they will never get to see grow up, to anyone who can't wake up from the Groundhog Day they're forced to live every day, to anyone who's marriage or family blew apart because of the stress of Caregiving I want to say, I'm sorry.

I'm sorry for the heartache you will have to experience. I'm sorry you have to walk the journey that is ahead of you. I'm sorry for the way you will have to feel during the most difficult times. But that's not all I want to tell you. I want to tell you that I applaud you. I want to tell you are doing a GREAT JOB. I want to tell you what you're doing is not going unnoticed. I want to tell you that you WILL be able to do ALL that is asked of you. I want to tell you it will be worth it in the end. I want to tell you that you're not alone. I want to tell you that all you've given up, will one day be given back to you, multiplied many times over. I want to tell you that God is the answer for every problem you will ever face in your life. Nothing is so broke, God's love cannot mend it back. Please remember that.

When you go through deep waters, I will be with you. When you go through rivers of difficulty, you will not drown. When you walk through the fire of oppression, you will not be burned up; the flames will not consume you.
Isaiah 43:2

I can happily lay my head down on my pillow at night and be able to say I have no regrets or feelings of guilt. I've done everything that was asked of me, with a willing heart. I know I've walked every step of my journey with God's Grace and Mercy as my guide. I may have stumbled and tripped alone the way, but God's Hand was always there to catch me before I fell.

I will always cling to the last precious moments I spent with my dad and my mom. Those last moments I poured out my heart to them. I wanted them to remember everything. I wanted them to remember the things we did together as a family. I wanted them to remember the things they taught me. I wanted them to remember the kind of wife and mother I had become. I wanted them to remember the influence they had on all of our lives. I wanted them to remember all the hugs and kisses. I wanted them to remember how special they made each of us feel. I wanted them to remember life. I wanted them to remember laughter. I wanted them to remember the fun they had with their grandchildren.

Most of all, I wanted my dad and my mom to remember the one thing I will never, ever forget. I know I will never forget, because my heart tied a string around my finger to make sure I will always remember. Most of all, I wanted my mom and dad "to remember love."

So you see, my story really has no end. Now, I will be able to move forward and live my life out loud, with a rich bounty of Peace and Joy to carry as my harvest, knowing I did everything I could have and should have to keep the last two promises I made to my parents. I will continue striving to daily live like Jesus, all the while knowing the most important thing He wants us to do is "to remember love."

For I can do everything through Christ,

who gives me strength.

Philippians 4:13

<u>My Footprint In Time</u>
© 2011 Tonya Ferguson

I sing what I live. My life becomes my songs.
Every word that I write down only makes me strong.
Each word, every note, is a mountain I've climbed.
Each word, every note, is my footprint in time.

Sometimes I could not laugh. Sometimes my joy ran deep.
Every line in every song, echos part of me.
Each word, every note, is a mountain I've climbed.
Each word, every note, is my footprint in time.

My days have turned to years. I've lived through many things.
One thing that I've come to know, while I live I'll sing.
Each word, every note, is a mountain I've climbed.
Each word, every note, is my footprint in time.

My heart cries out. I have no doubt He'll answer.
I hold the pen, the words are written by the very hand of God.
Each word, every note, is a mountain I've climbed.
Each word, every note, is my footprint in time.

I sing what I live. My life becomes my songs.
Every word that I write down only makes me strong.
That's my footprint in time.

From My Caregiving Heart, To Yours

Just because my Caregiving experience happened to deal with Alzheimer's, doesn't mean this book can't speak to the heart of ALL CAREGIVERS. Caregiving is Caregiving. It doesn't matter what the condition is of the person that you are caring for.

Just because I talk about being a Caregiver, doesn't mean this book can't speak to the heart of friends or family of Caregivers. There are lessons to be learned for anyone who reads these pages.

This book is for anyone who has an ear to hear and a heart to feel. I don't think anyone willl read this book and not be able to think of at least one person that could benefit from reading it. That's how widespread this epidemic of Caregiving has become.

Before your life is over you WILL fall into one of two categories. You will either be a Caregiver, or a friend or family member of a Caregiver. Either way, Caregiving WILL touch your life at some point, in some way.

Finally, I want to leave you all with these two letters:

To All My Dear, Fellow Caregivers,

You may be Caregiving for a baby born Prematurely or with Birth Defects, someone who has had a Stroke, a child with Autism, someone who has Cancer, someone who has Cystic Fibrosis, someone who has Heart Disease, someone who has Multiple Sclerosis, someone with Down's Syndrome, someone who has a Brain Injury, someone who has Parkinson's Disease, someone who has A.L.S., someone who has Huntington's Disease, someone who has AIDS, someone that is in a Coma, someone with Mental Illness, someone who has a Spinal Cord Injury, someone with Chronic Disabling Pain, someone who has Emphysema, or any number of other diseases or conditions. The bottom line is you are sacrificing your own life to give unconditional love and be a Caregiver for someone that's been placed in your life. You may not understand "Why" now, but just know that GOD WILL HONOR WHAT YOU'RE DOING!

You may not have had any time to prepare for becoming a Caregiver. You may not have even been asked if you wanted to be a Caregiver. You may never have thought you would ever have to be a Caregiver. Nevertheless, you ARE a Caregiver. Some things we ask for. Some things are just given to us.

You may only be a Caregiver for a few weeks or months. Or maybe you'll be a Caregiver for years and years. No matter what, your life is not your own because you are a Caregiver.

I remember reading that being a Caregiver is extremely hard on your health and extremely stressful. I don't think I fully understood that until after my mom went to Heaven. Up to that point I never allowed myself to think about "me" long enough, during my 9 ½ years of Caregiving, to feel the true impact of the stress. It certainly was inside me, but I never allowed myself to communicate with it.

I read where Caregivers should take care of themselves, accept help from friends and family, take time off to get away for a while, commit to staying healthy, stay connected socially with friends, and on and on and on. In a perfect world that would have been great. It didn't take me long to realize that all of those things would have been extremely helpful and it all sounded very logical when I read it, but I found it impossible to implement those things into my life. In a very short amount of time I could see that those things were not going to be a part of my Caregiving life. So I just learned to adapt to what my reality was. That's what I do when I'm given lemons. I make lemonade.

I am here to tell you, with or without those things in your life, you CAN and WILL survive being a Caregiver. I know this because I did. Sure, I encountered a few war wounds along the way and will forever carry the scars, but I am so much stronger, in so many ways, than I was before I was a Caregiver. Unfortunately, I was not able to have those things in my Caregiving experience. Would it have made it a little easier at times? You'd better believe it. But I can't miss what I didn't have. I can't live it any differently than I did. What was then is then. What is now is now. That's Life. I don't get a "Do-Over."

What you are chosing to do as a Caregiver is honorable, and even talked about in the Bible. What you are doing is laying down your life for the sake of putting someone else's life first. You are saying their needs are more important than your own. You are living a selfless life. You are proving that you are willing to sacrifice your wants and needs to see that someone else's wants and needs are met. It takes someone really special to do that. You are doing an awesome thing. You are giving an incredible gift. Never forget that. Even if you never hear the words "Thank You." NEVER FORGET THAT!

Until the next time we talk...Stand on Philippians 4:13.

Love, Hugs, & Prayers,

Tonya

This is my commandment:
Love each other in the same way I have loved you.
There is no greater love than to lay down one's life
for one's friends.
John 15:13-14

To All My Dear Friends of a Caregiver,

If you are reading this and you aren't a Caregiver but you have a friend or family member that is a Caregiver, HELP THEM. PLEASE, HELP THEM! Don't wait until they ask for help because that may never happen. No one wants to have to ask for help. No one wants to have to share their burdens with others. Trust me, THEY NEED HELP. What is giving a few hours out of your life, every once in a while, compared to the twenty-four hours a day, every day, your Caregiver friend gives up in their life?

Believe me when I tell you, your Caregiver friend WILL grow accustomed to the nightmare in which they are living. They may give the appearance they are doing fine. They may possibly even believe it themselves. They may tell you they don't need any help, but trust me, they do. They may even make Caregiving look so easy you don't see the need in offering them any help. Look beyond what you see and think about how they must be feeling.

If all you do is just give them someone else to talk to, to laugh with, or to cry with. If all you do is offer to sit with their loved one so they can go get their hair done, go to the doctor, go to a movie, go shopping, go for a walk, go to church, go take a class, or get a massage. If all you do is make it a point to go to the Caregiver's home and spend time with them there. I remember feeling so cut off from the world, right in my own home, because people didn't want to come to my house any more. If all you do is give them your time for their sake, it will be the most precious gift you will ever give to anyone. PLEASE, don't just ask them if you can do something, DO SOMETHING! You may think what you're doing is nothing, but it could be everything in the world of a Caregiver.

Reach out to them when they are too tired to take hold of your hand. Reach out to them when you can see the brokenness in their heart and spirit. Reach out to them and catch their tears as they fall from their eyes. Reach out to them and give them hugs they'll never ask for. Reach out to them and let them know they are loved. Reach out to them and SHOW them the LOVE of JESUS. Be the person you would want someone to be to you, if you were in their shoes. One day you may have to become a Caregiver too.

Until the next time we talk...Stand on Philippians 4:13.

Love, Hugs, & Prayers,

Tonya

This is my commandment:
Love each other in the same way I have loved you.
There is no greater love than to lay down one's life for one's friends.
John 15:13-14

to remember love

To anyone who sacrifices all, giving all you can each night and day.
A fragile life in need of constant care, gently in your life was placed.
I want to say I'm sorry, for the footsteps you must walk.
I want to say I'm sorry, when you feel all time has stopped.
Please hear me when I say, when minutes feel like days,
your love is on display.

When all you know is sleepless nights, when your tears fall down like rain.
When sorrow is your greatest friend, when no one sees your pain.
You try to wipe away each day, all the lost and broken dreams.
You pray the Lord their soul will keep, and see what tomorrow brings.

To anyone who sacrifices all, for the sake of someone else's life.
Days you give are turning into years, and your heart is full of grief inside.
I want to say I'm sorry, for the heartache you will know.
I want to say I'm sorry, when your darkness overflows.
Please hear me when I say, life you give away,
is your love on display.

When you struggle just to try and pray, when you're broken and afraid.
Know when stress is bearing down, new strength will come each day.
Your heart will break a thousand times, as you watch them fight their fight.
But think how dark their life would be, without your shining light.

I want to say I'm sorry, cause I've lived what you're living through.
I want to say I'm sorry, cause I've walked where you're walking too.
So hear me when I say, you won't regret a day, your love was on display.

Please know that I applaud you now, for the care you give each day.
You're doing all that's asked of you, in the most unselfish way.
So as you let your mind erase, all the things you've given up.
The one thing you must not forget, is to remember love.

No matter how it ends, the one gift you must give yourself,
is to remember love.

Some of my most valuable Life Lessons have been revealed to me through my trials and tears.

The finest China in the world is fired, or burned, at least three times. It takes that many times to bring out the "Utmost Beauty" of that fine piece of China.

Sometimes a Life Lesson was fired, or burned into me one time. Others took two times. Then there were those that took three times or more.

Just like the finest China, I am being fashioned in each fire I have to endure, to bring out my "Utmost Beauty." Only God can do that. Only God can give me "Beauty For The Ashes."

My Story Has No End...

ARRIVING IN EARLY 2012

MY NEW CD

"to remember love"

The entire time I was writing this book I was also busy writing songs and working on recording those songs for my new CD, "to remember love." The songs on this CD have an entirely different flavor than the songs I've written before. They came from a new place in my heart.

I live the songs I sing. I always have, and always will. So I guess as my life began to change after my mom went to Heaven, it also caused my songs to begin to change. These new songs were written at the end of a vicious, thirteen year storm. While I was writing them I noticed a glimmer of healing stirring in my heart. At the end of my storm, I finally began to feel like I was living life under a clear blue sky, with God's rainbow to light the path of my new journey.

My CD, "to remember love," is what this book would sound like if it were put to music. They both go hand in hand.

To get my CD "to remember love" go to:
www.amazon.com or itunes.
You will also be able to get it through my website at
www.tonya-ferguson.com.

CPSIA information can be obtained at www.ICGtesting.com
Printed in the USA
LVOW112133070212

267619LV00003B/21/P

9 780984 777204